A Comparative Study

by J.A. Cook

Fade To Black

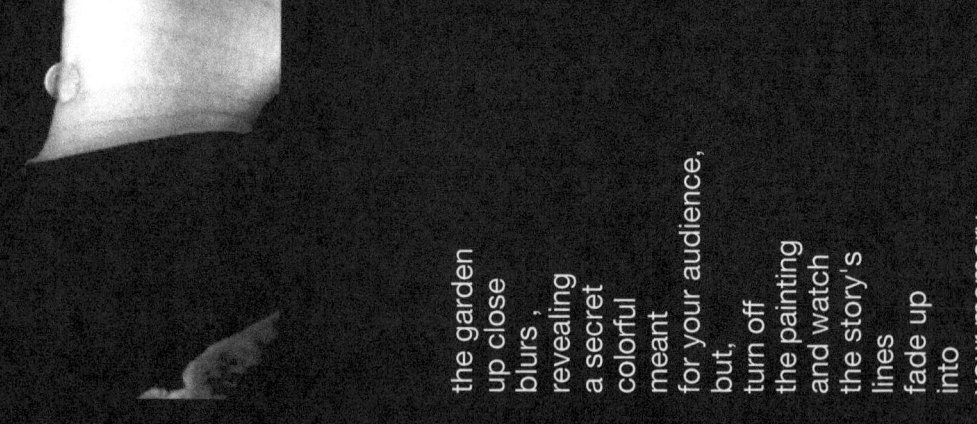

the garden
up close
blurs ,
revealing
a secret
colorful
meant
for your audience,
but,
turn off
the painting
and watch
the story's
lines
fade up
into
your memory

Fade To Black

Images by J.A. Cook

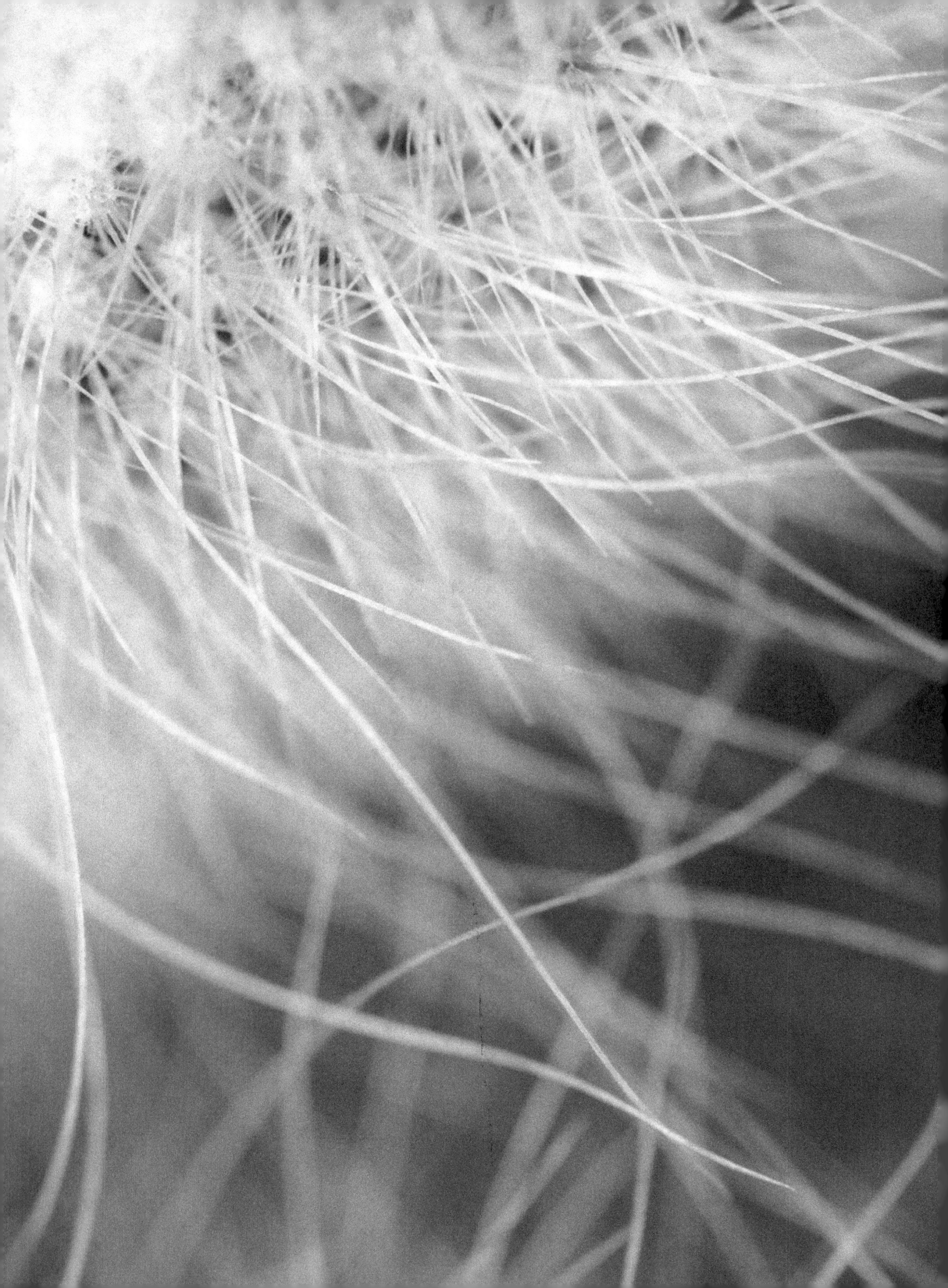

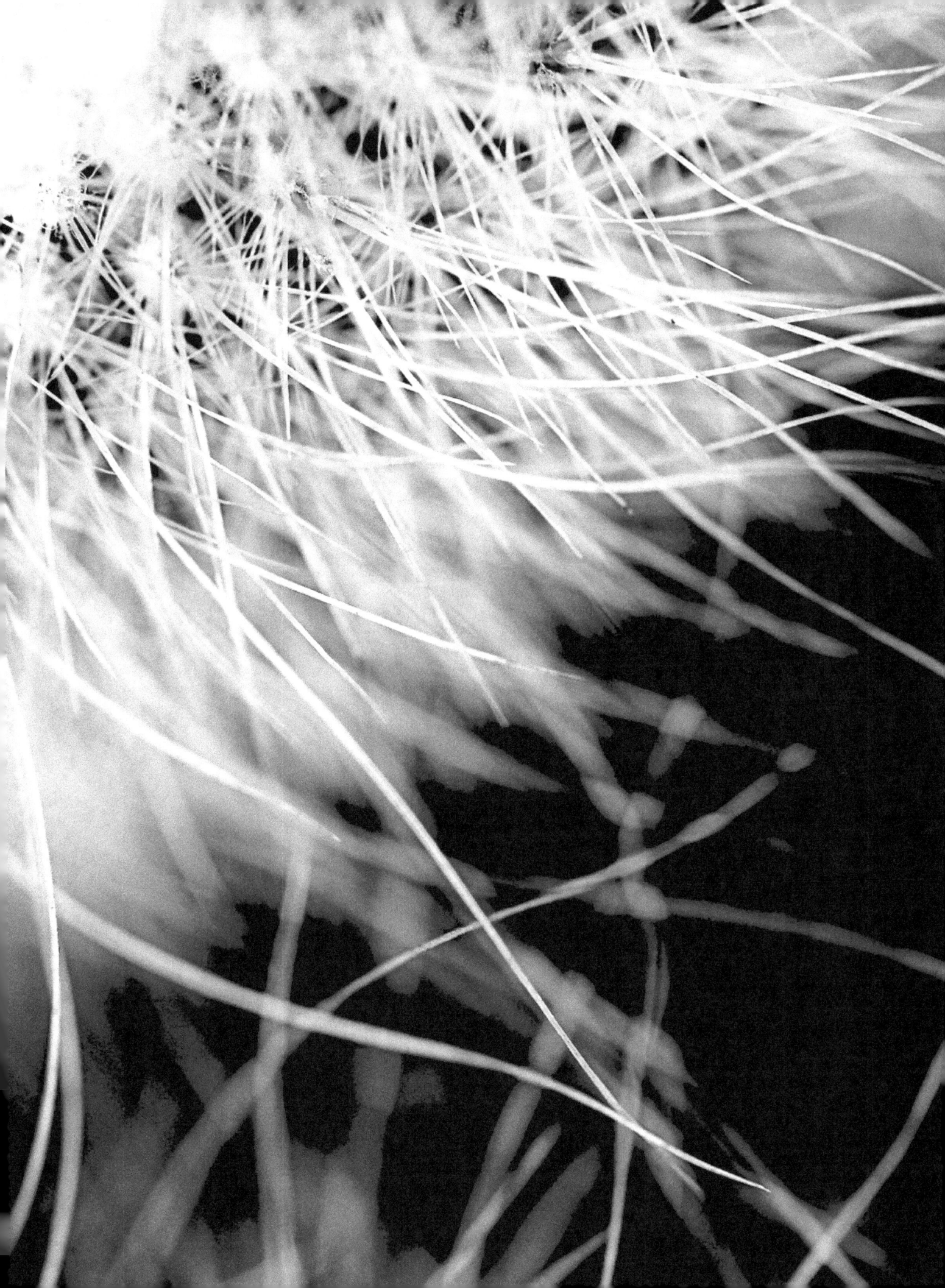

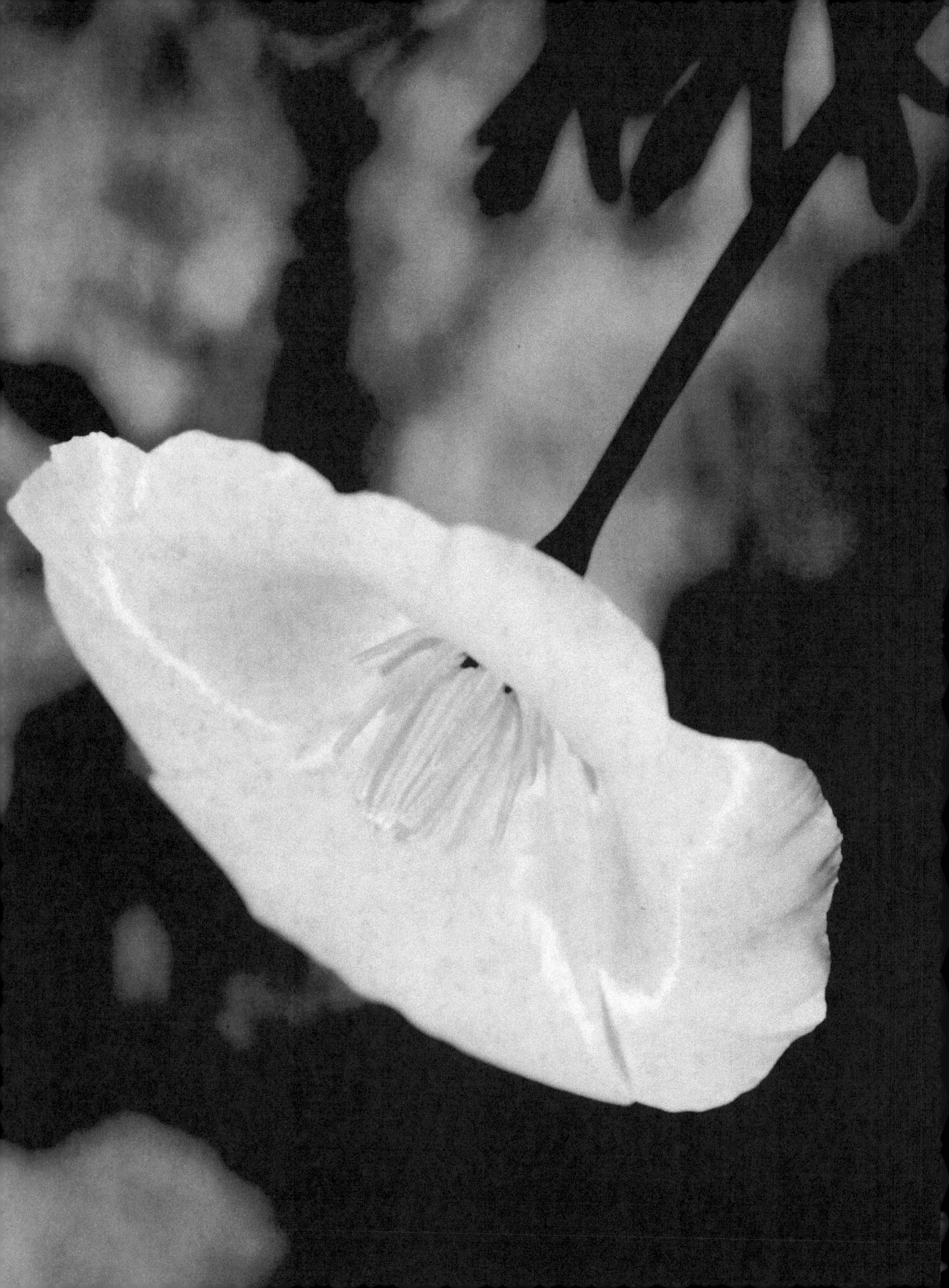

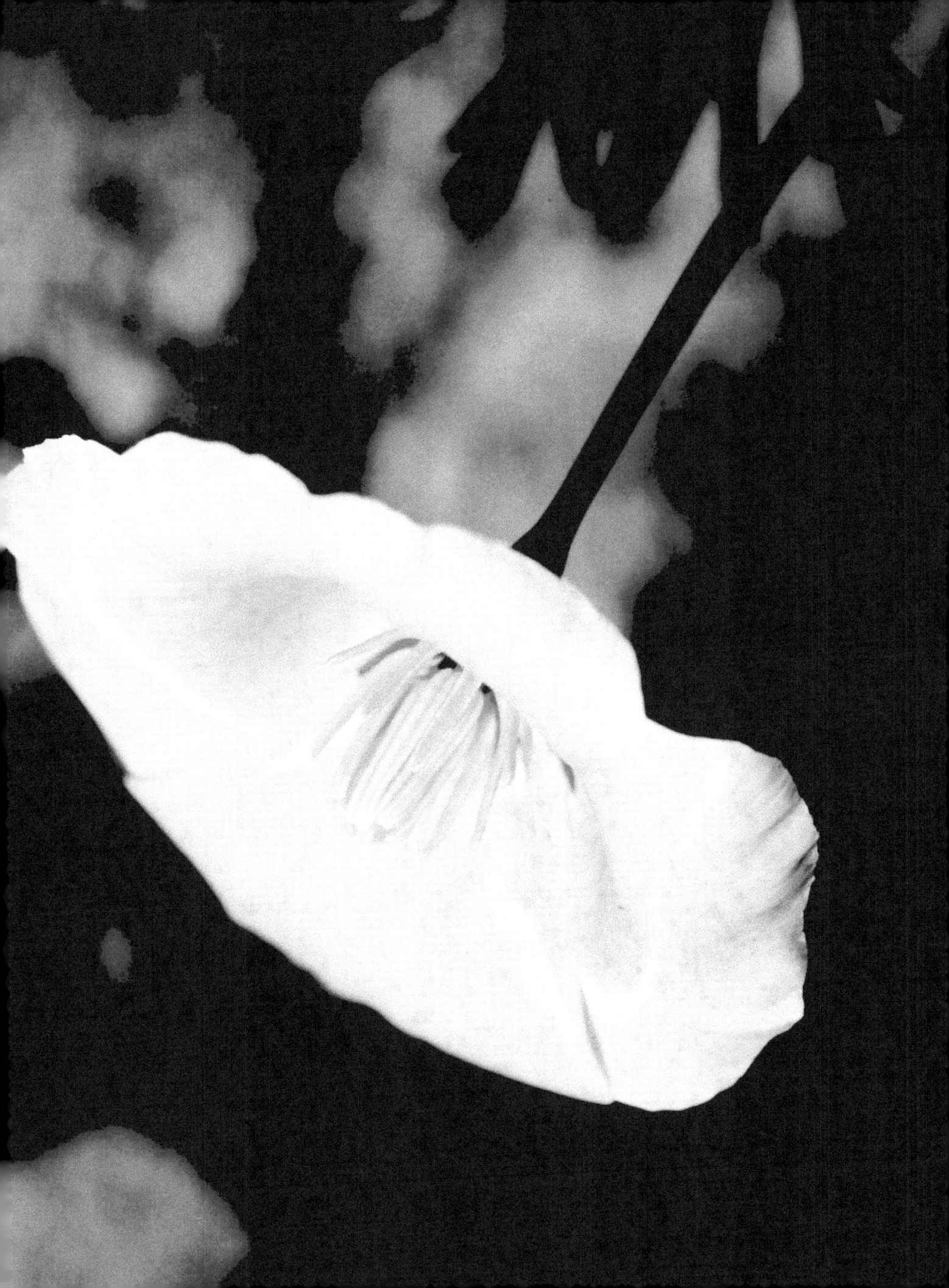

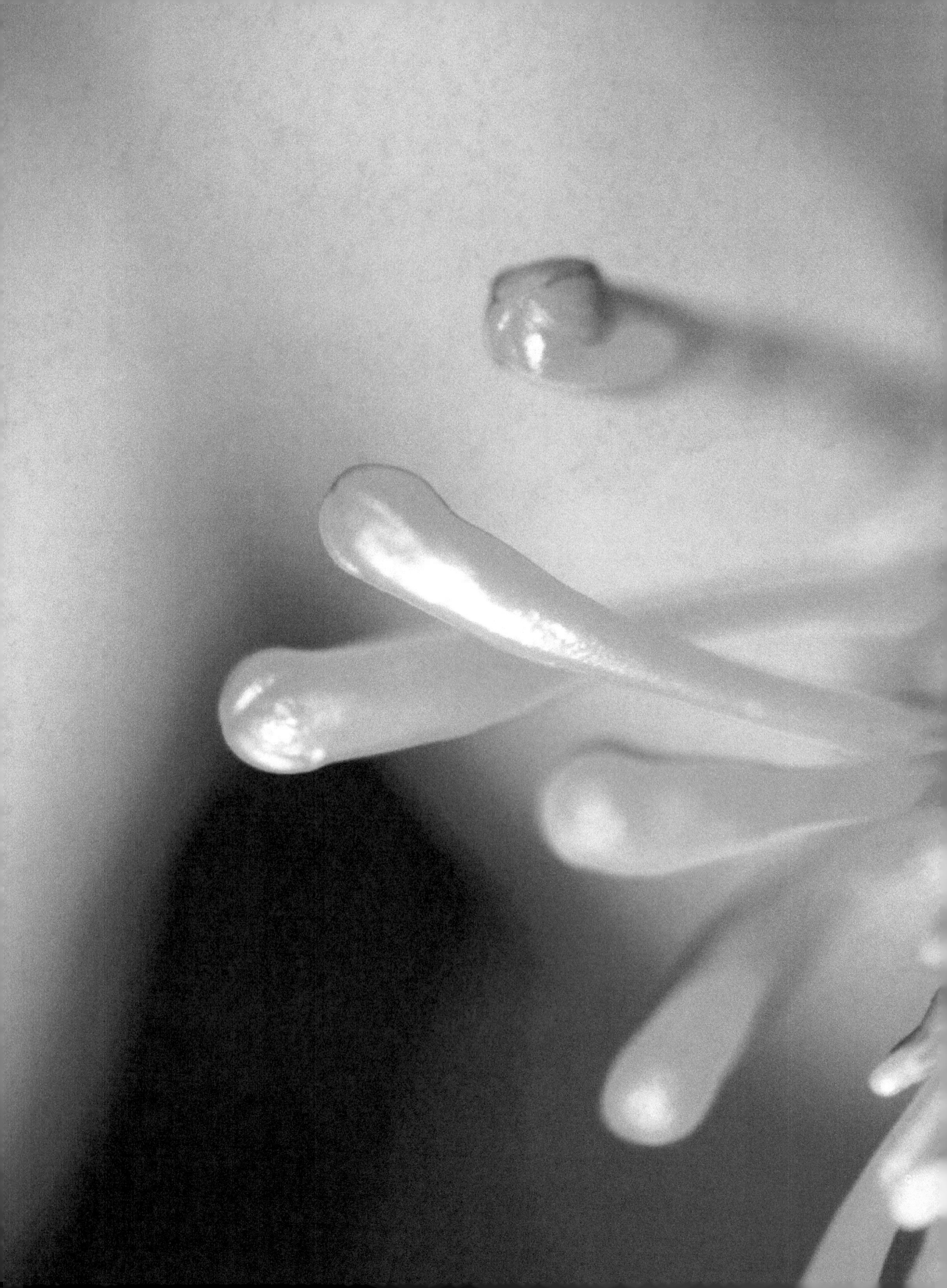

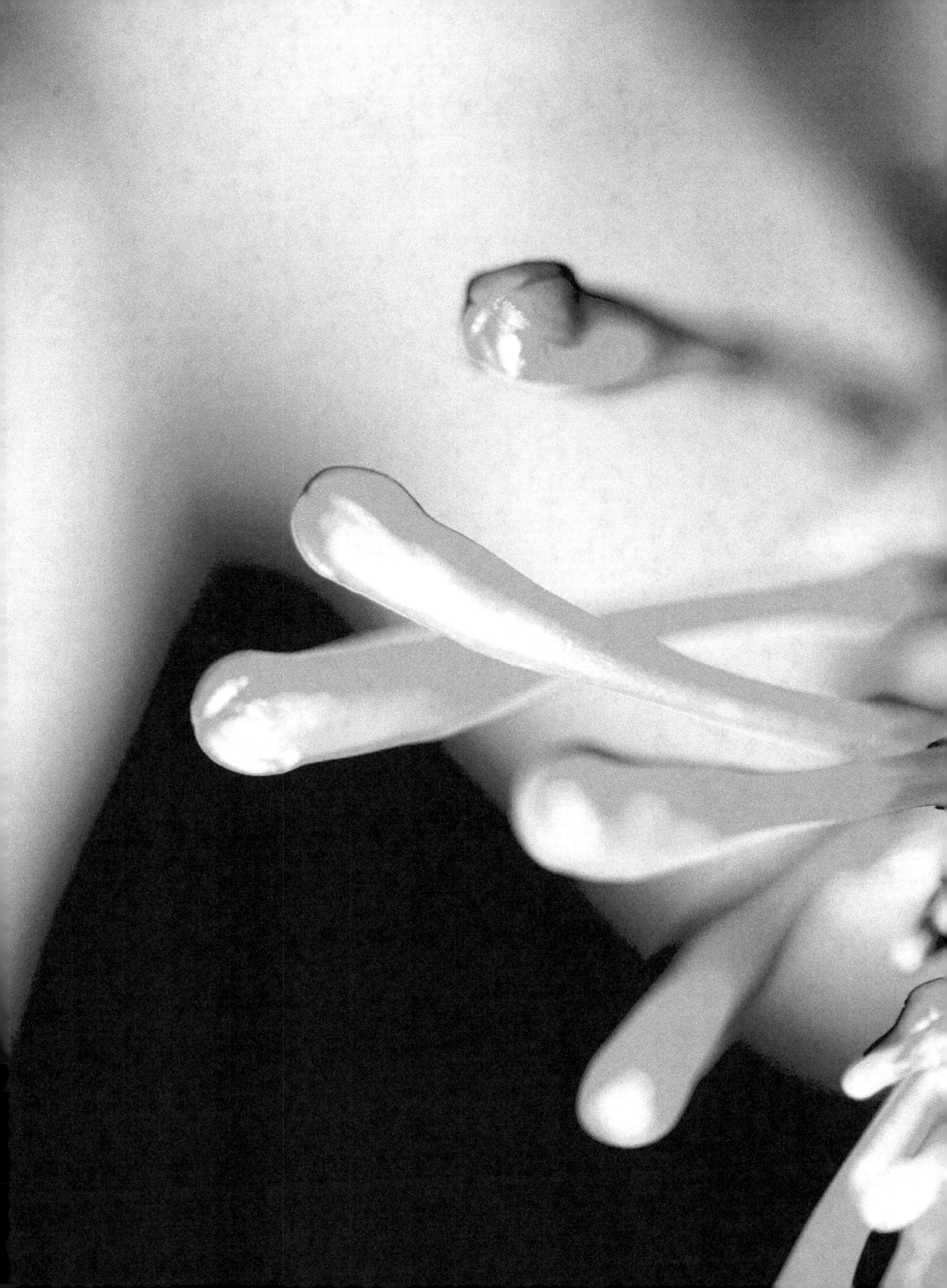

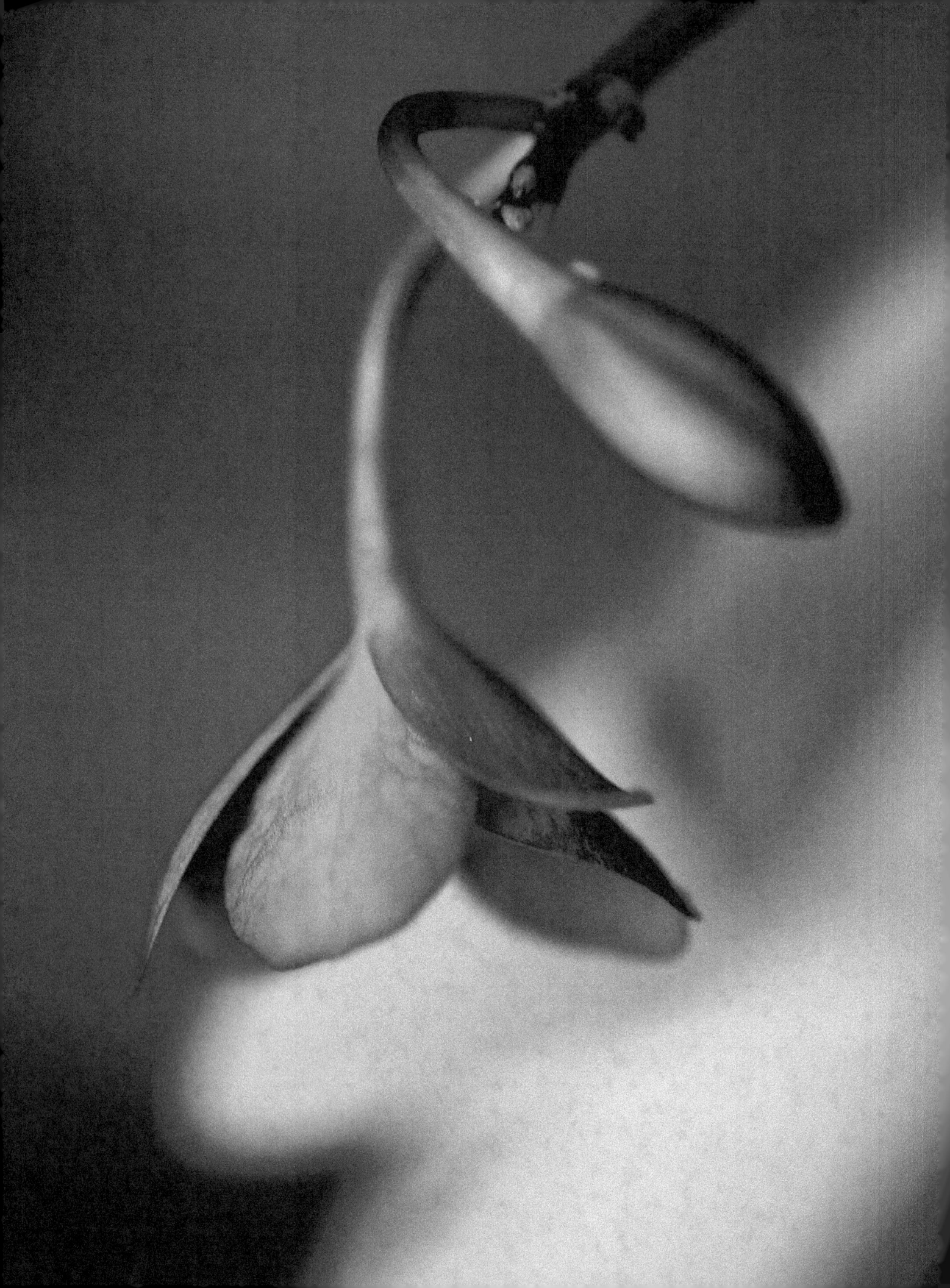

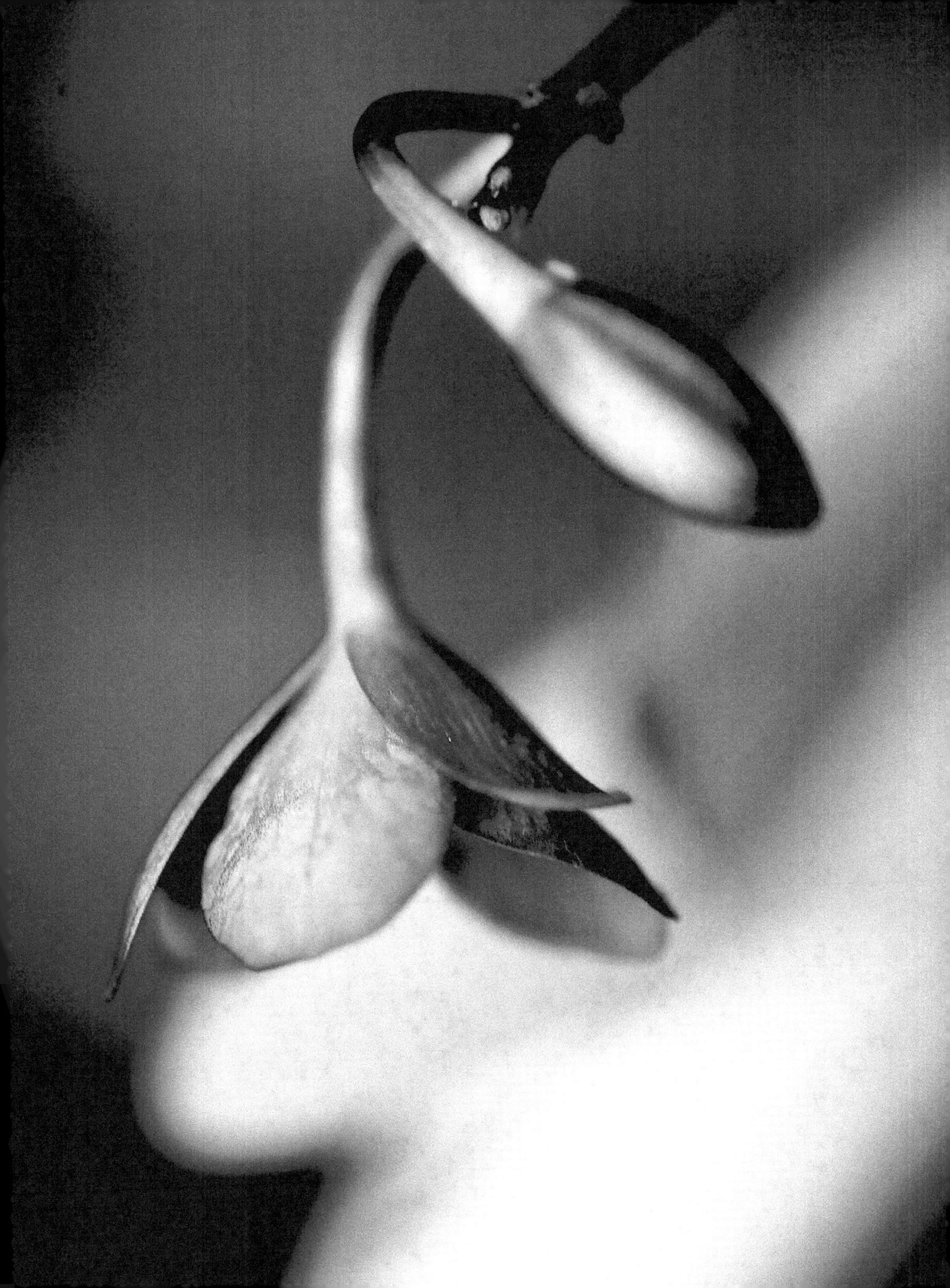

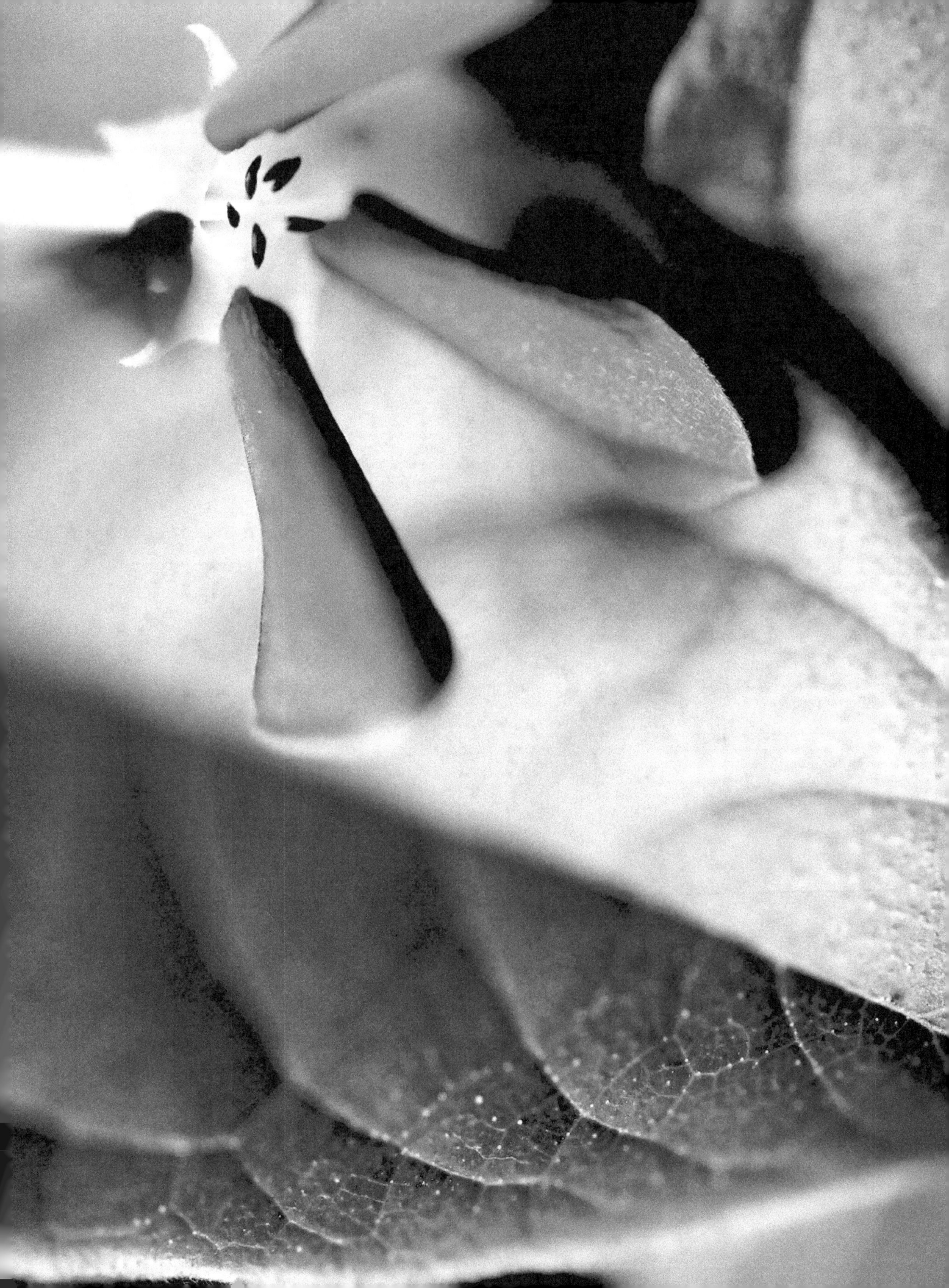

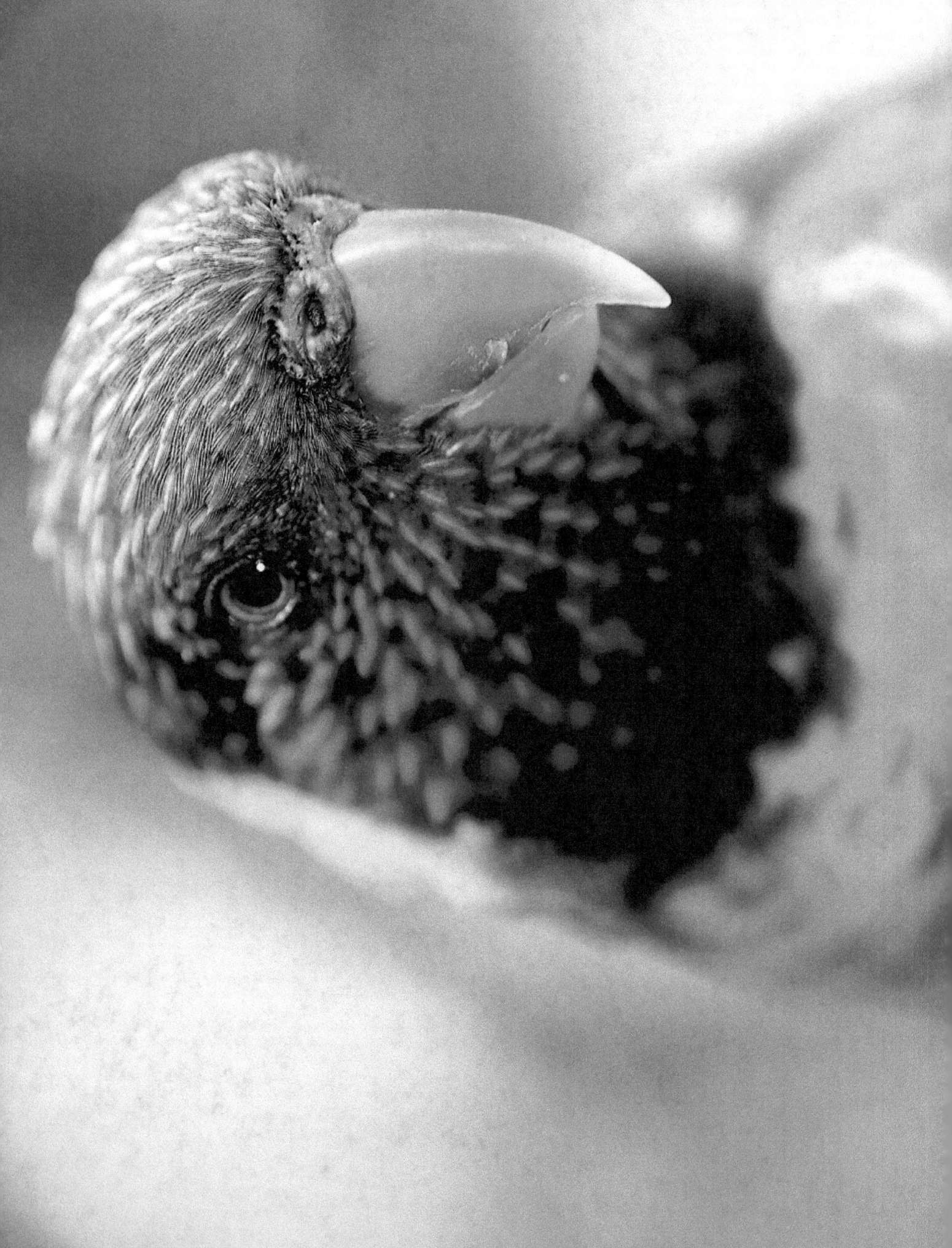

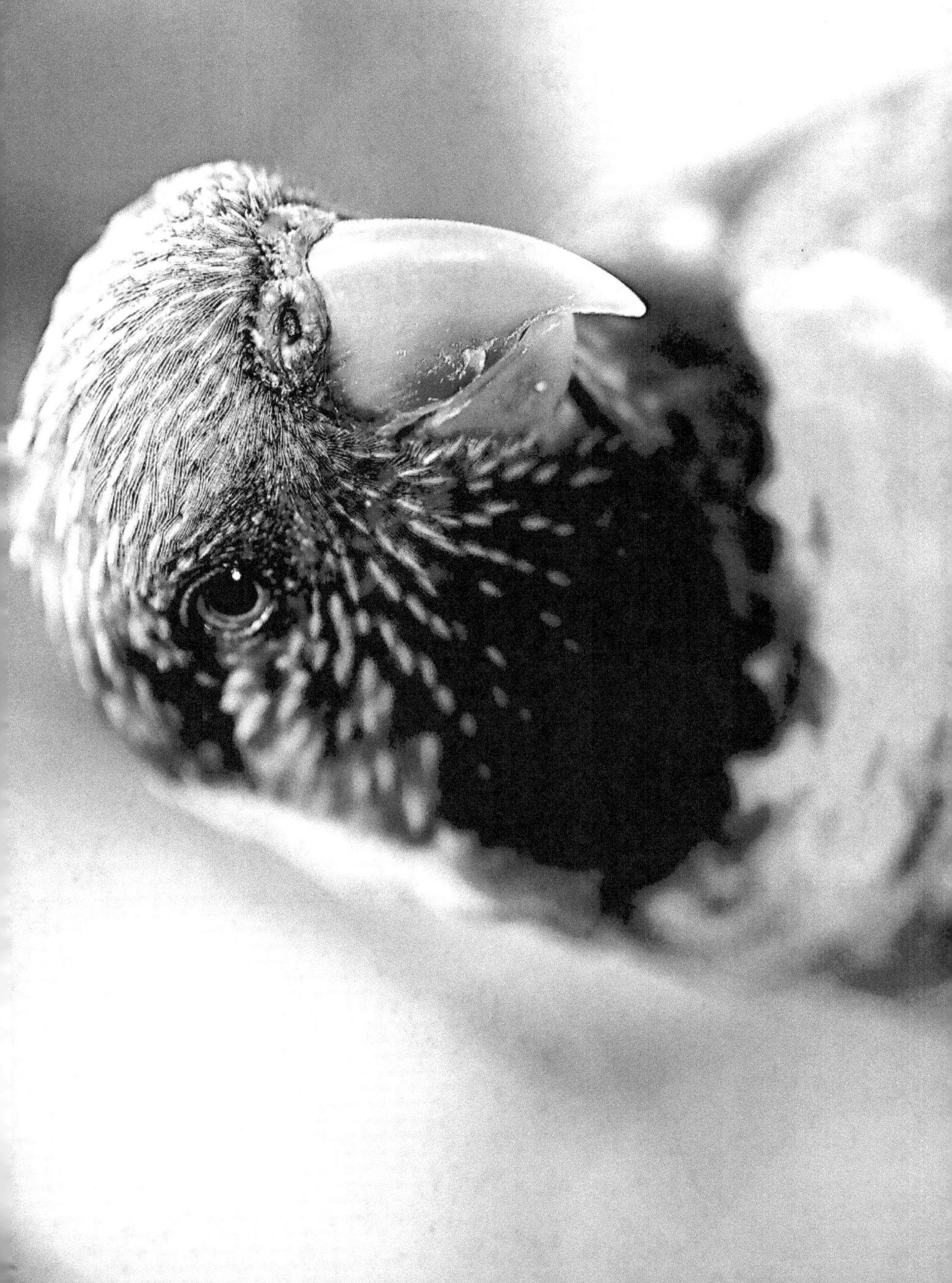

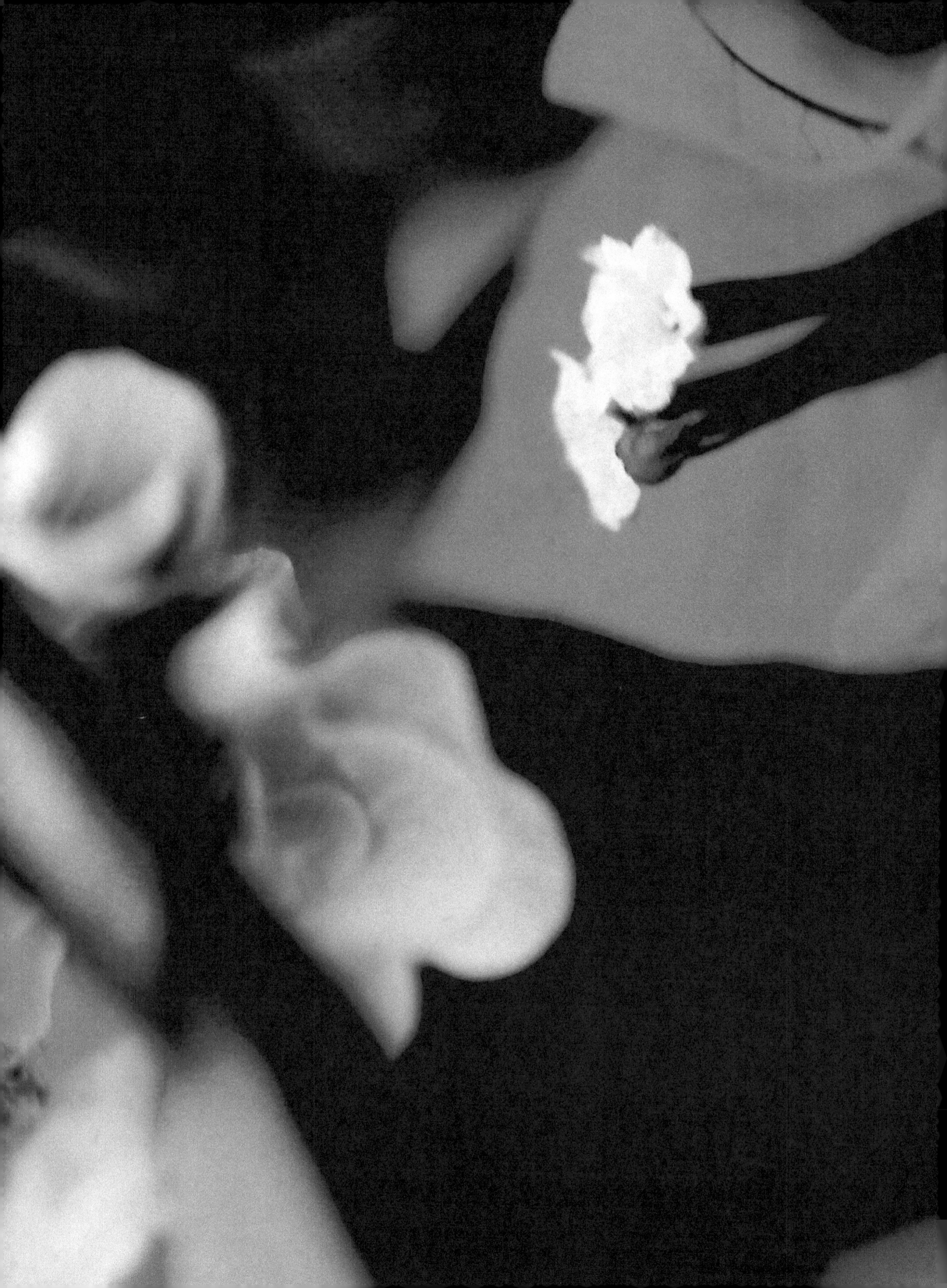

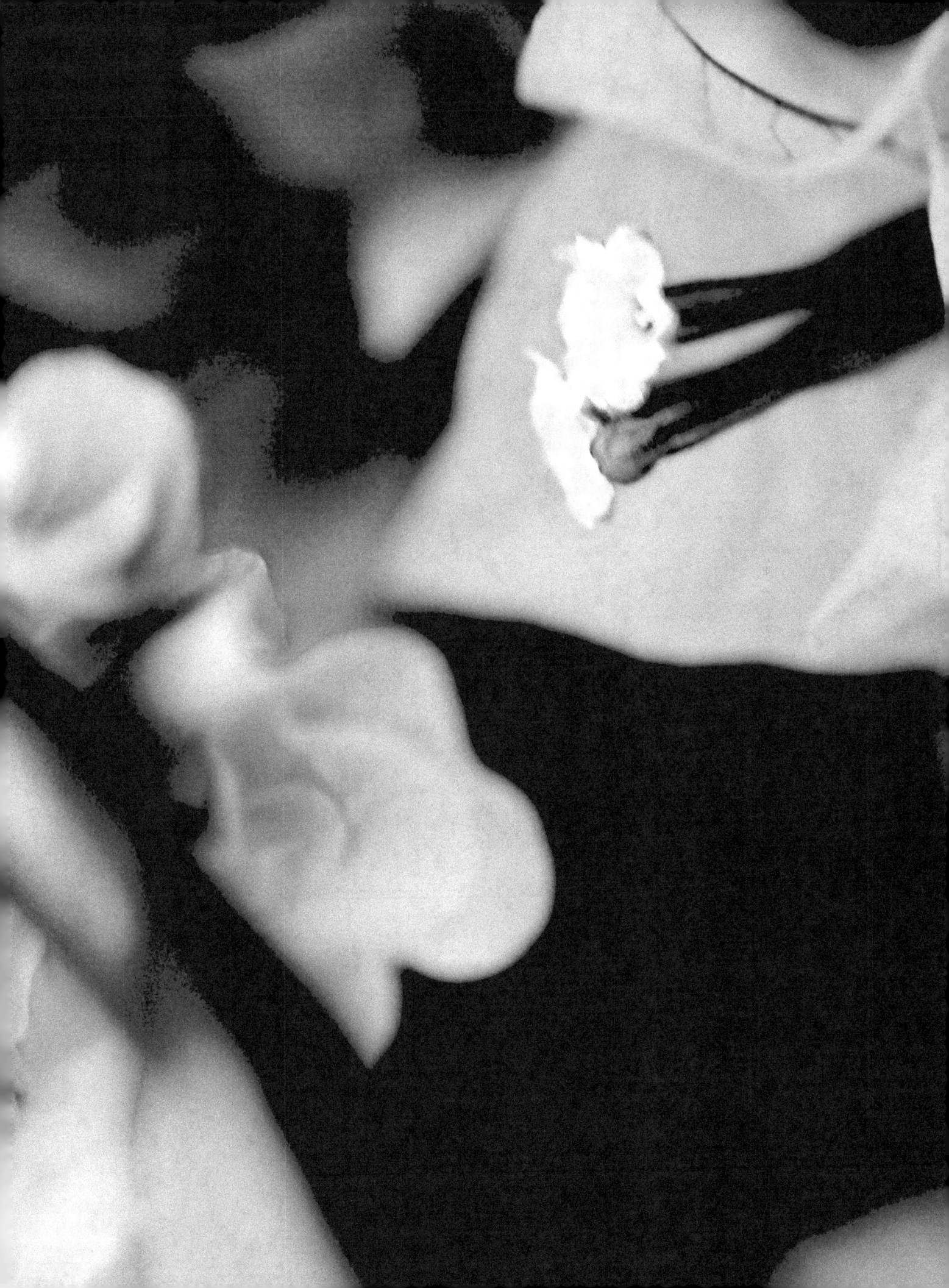

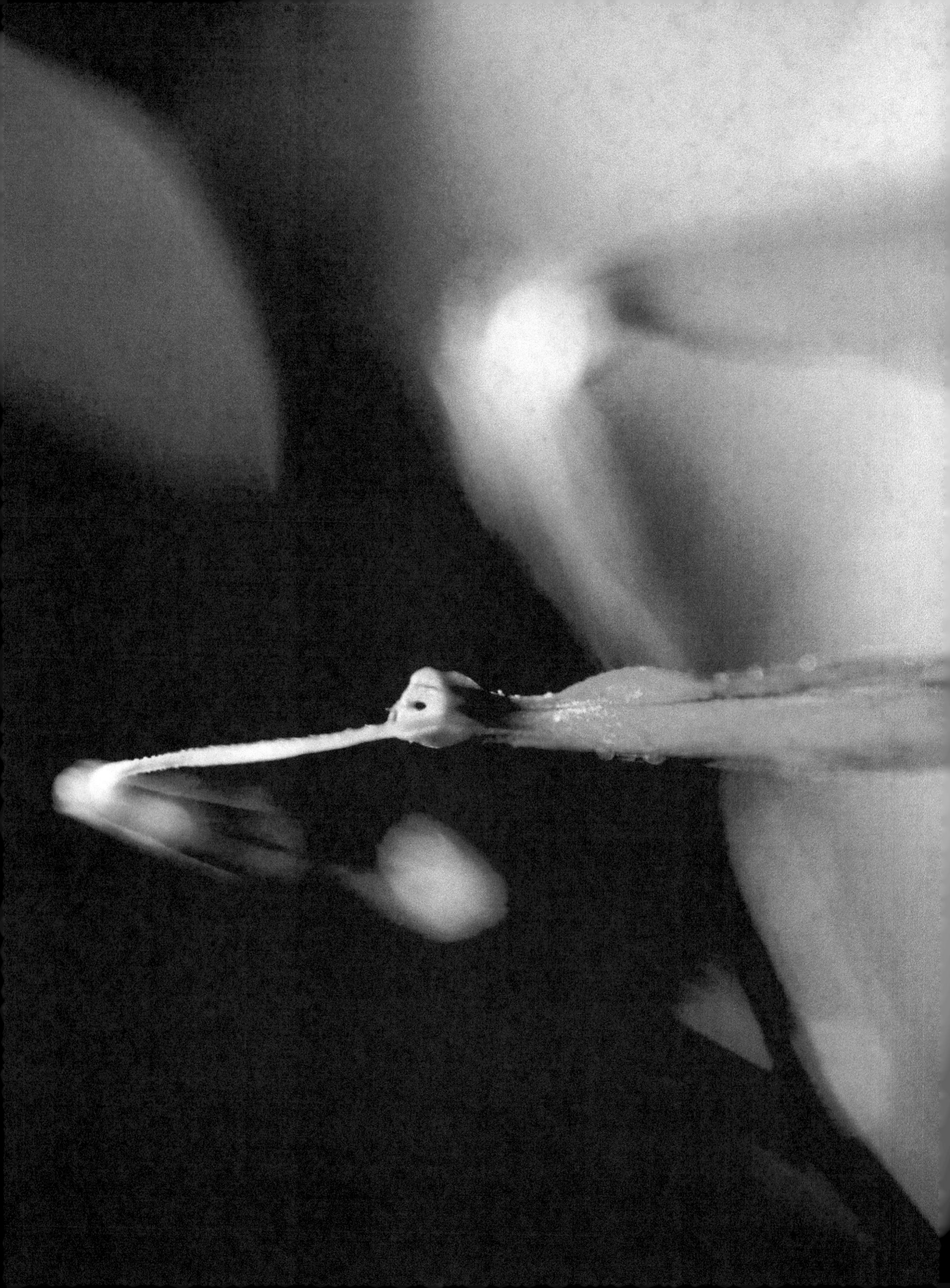

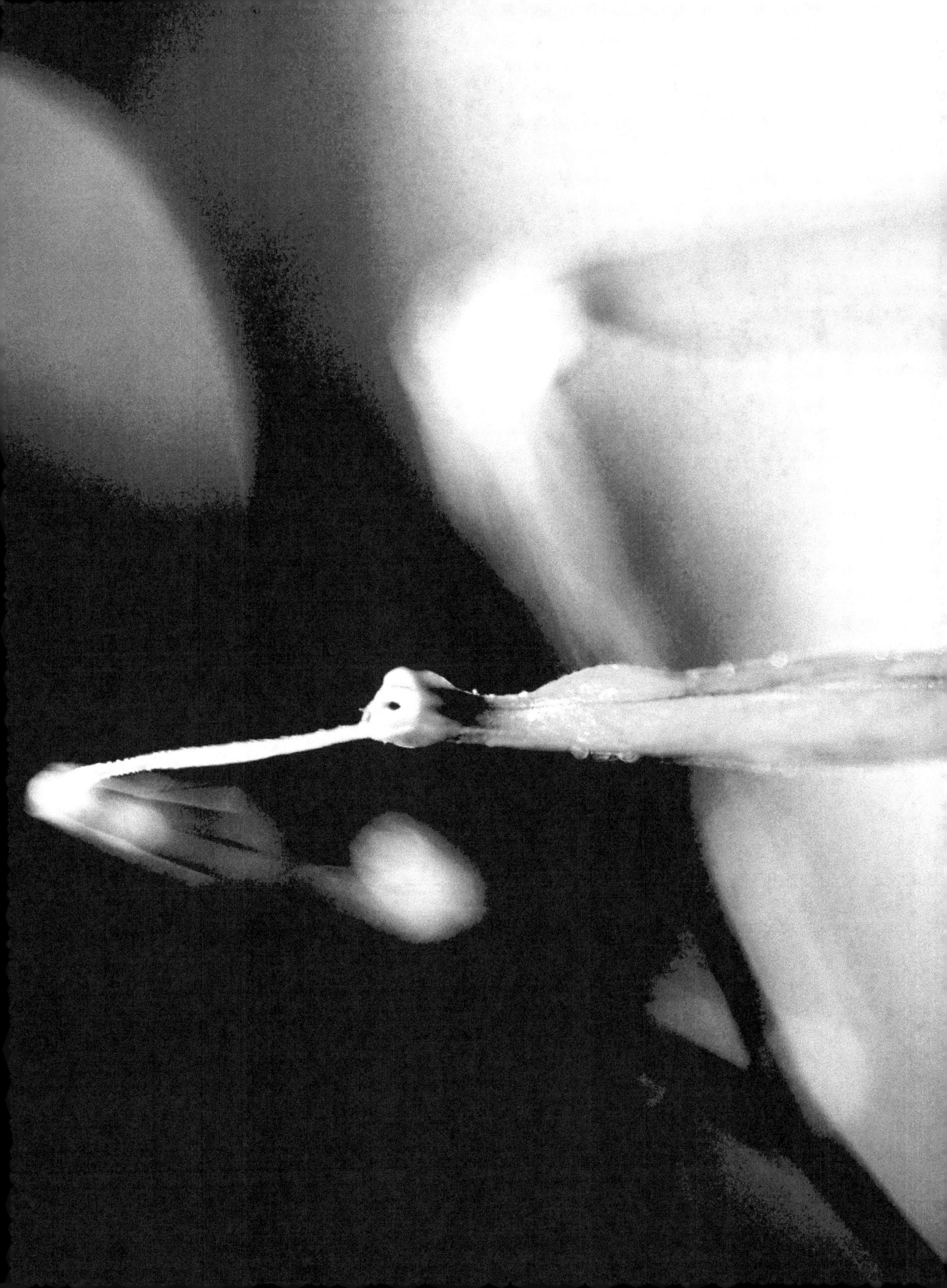

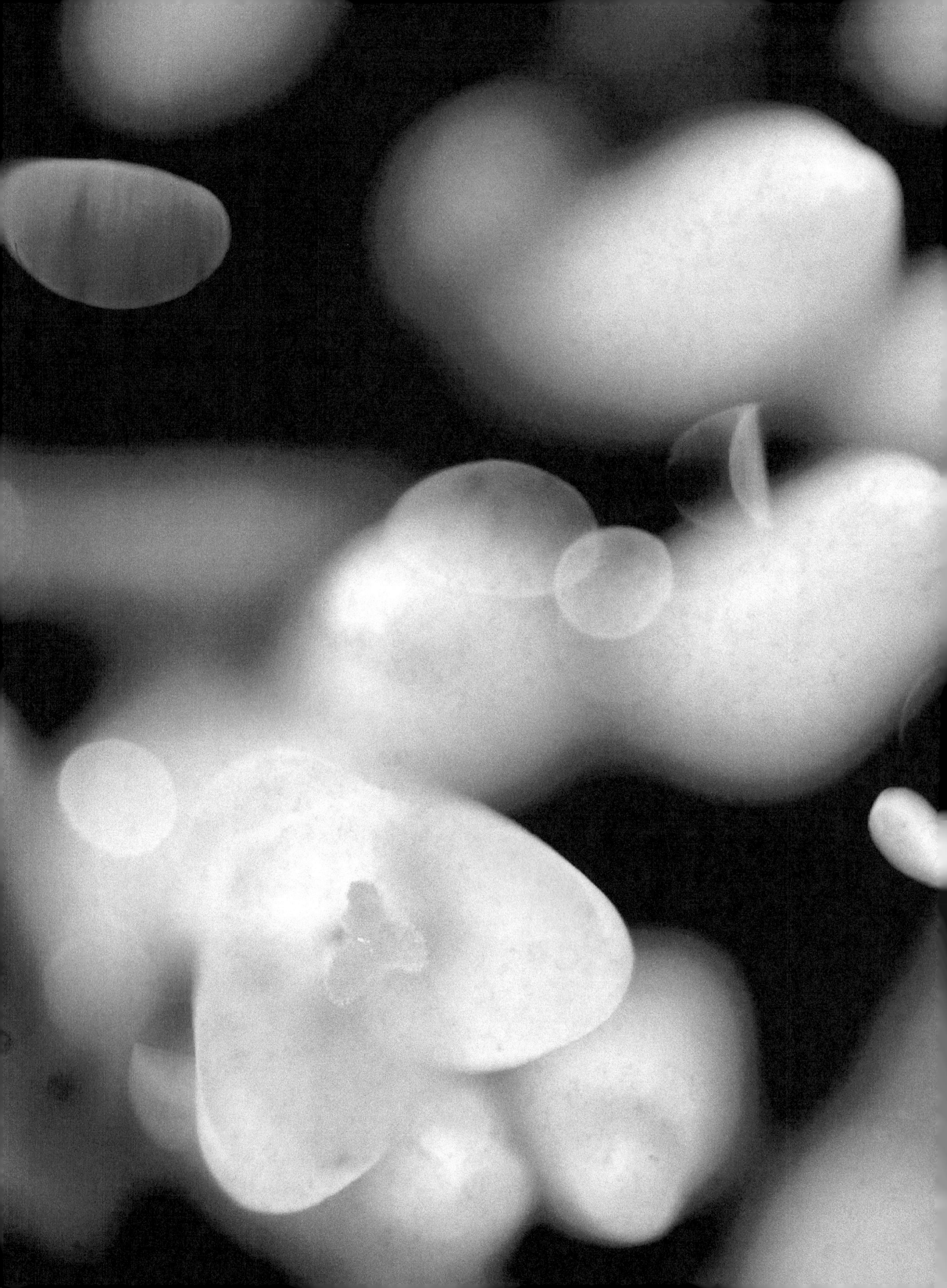

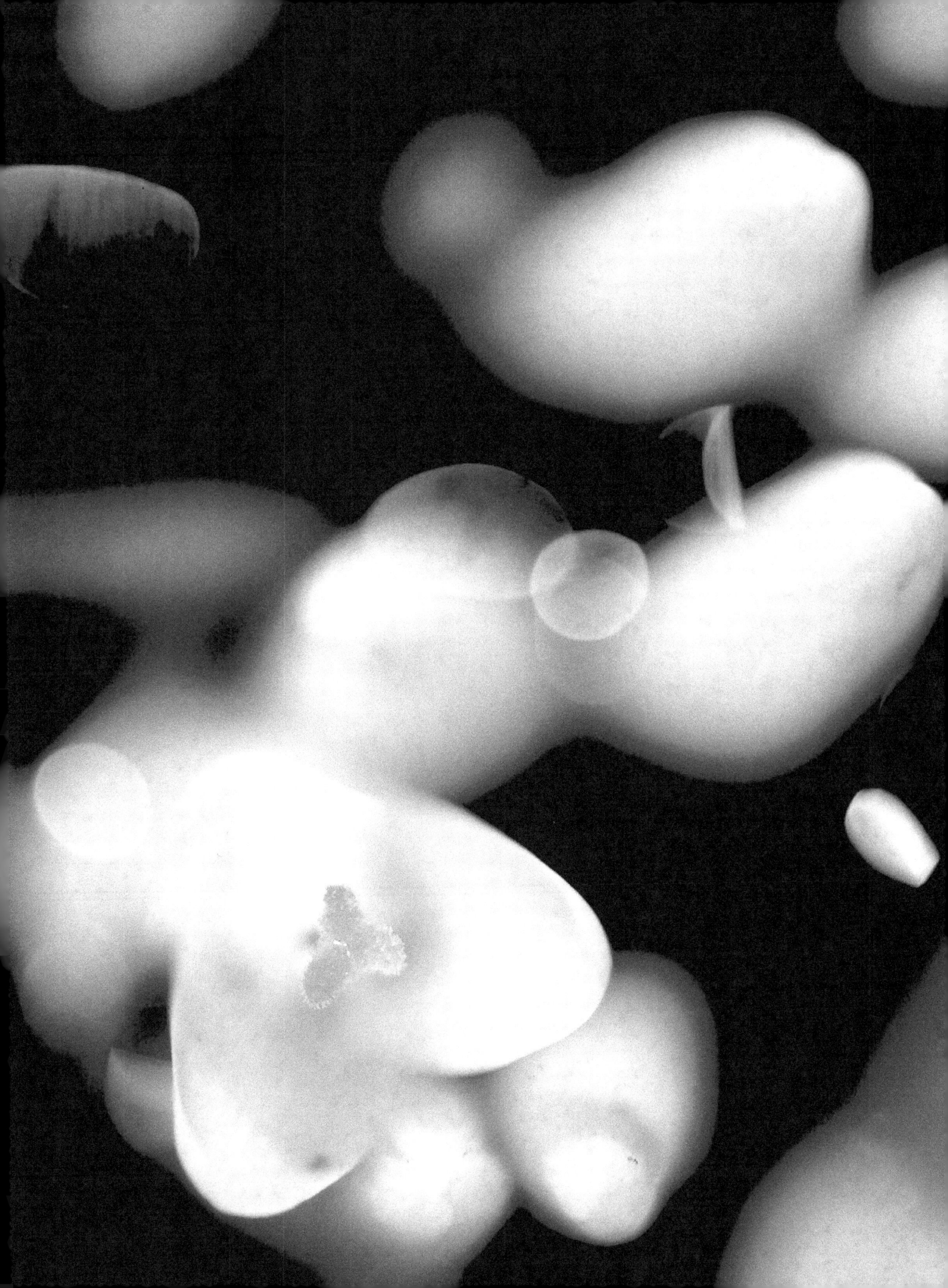

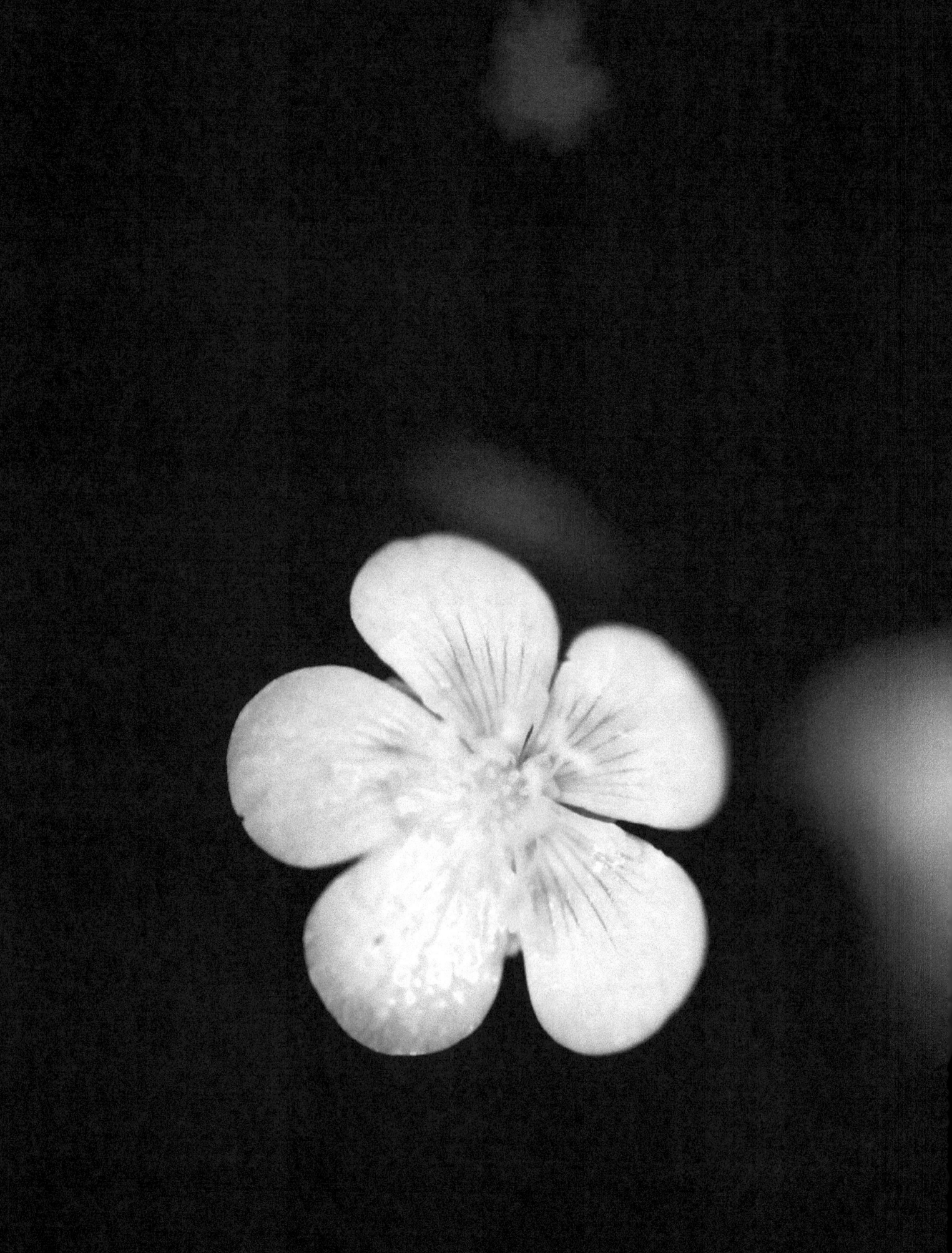

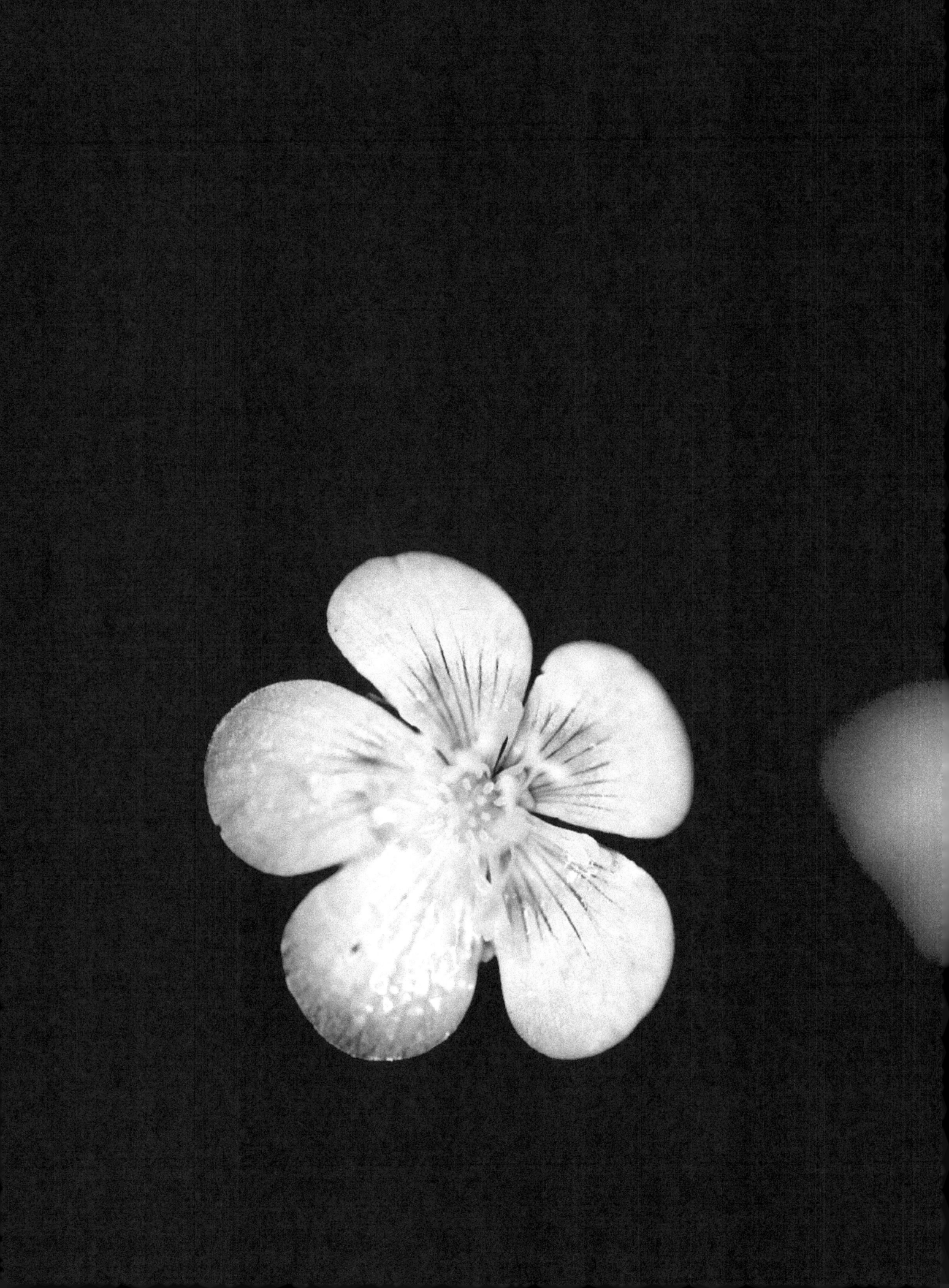

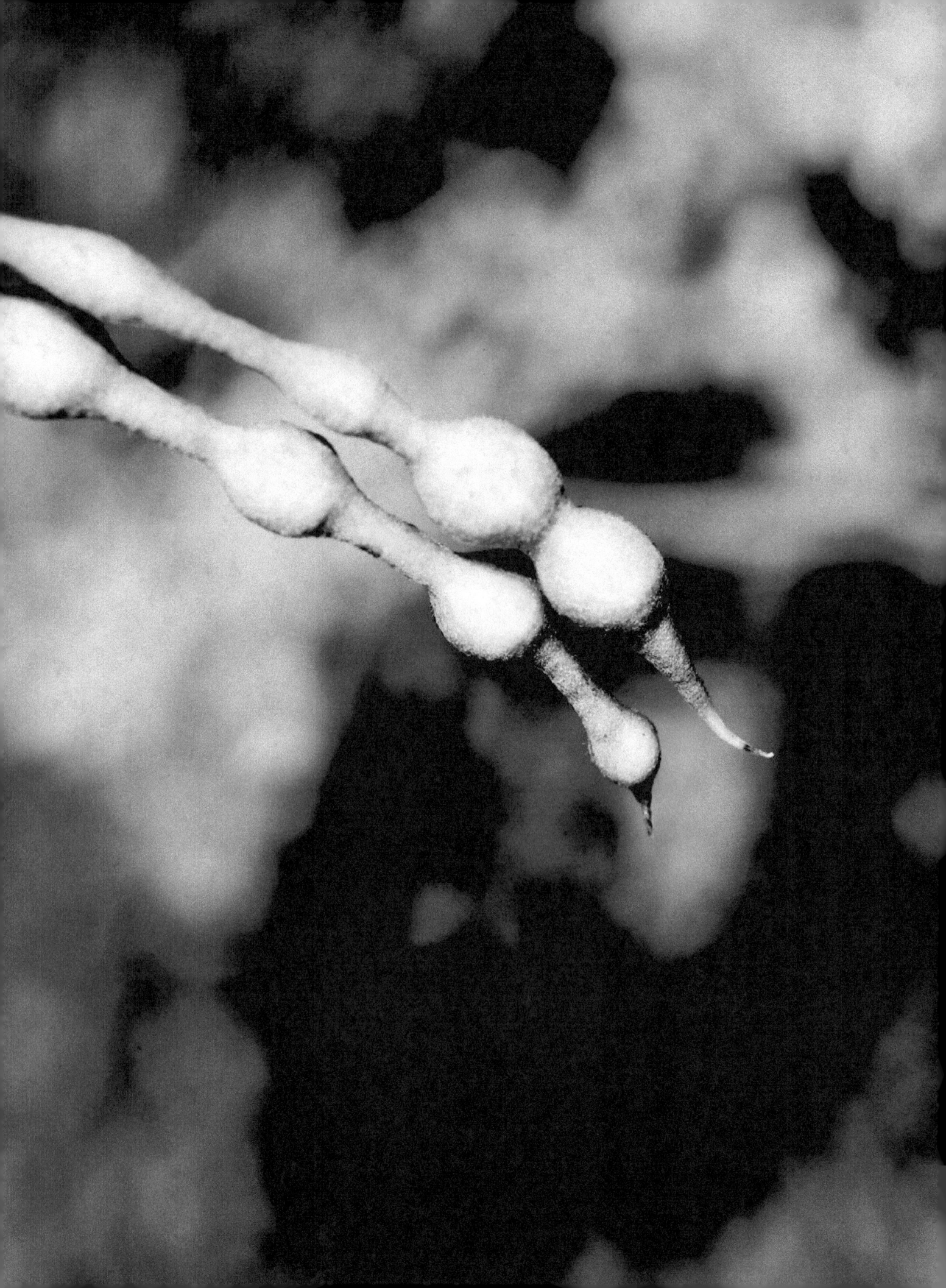

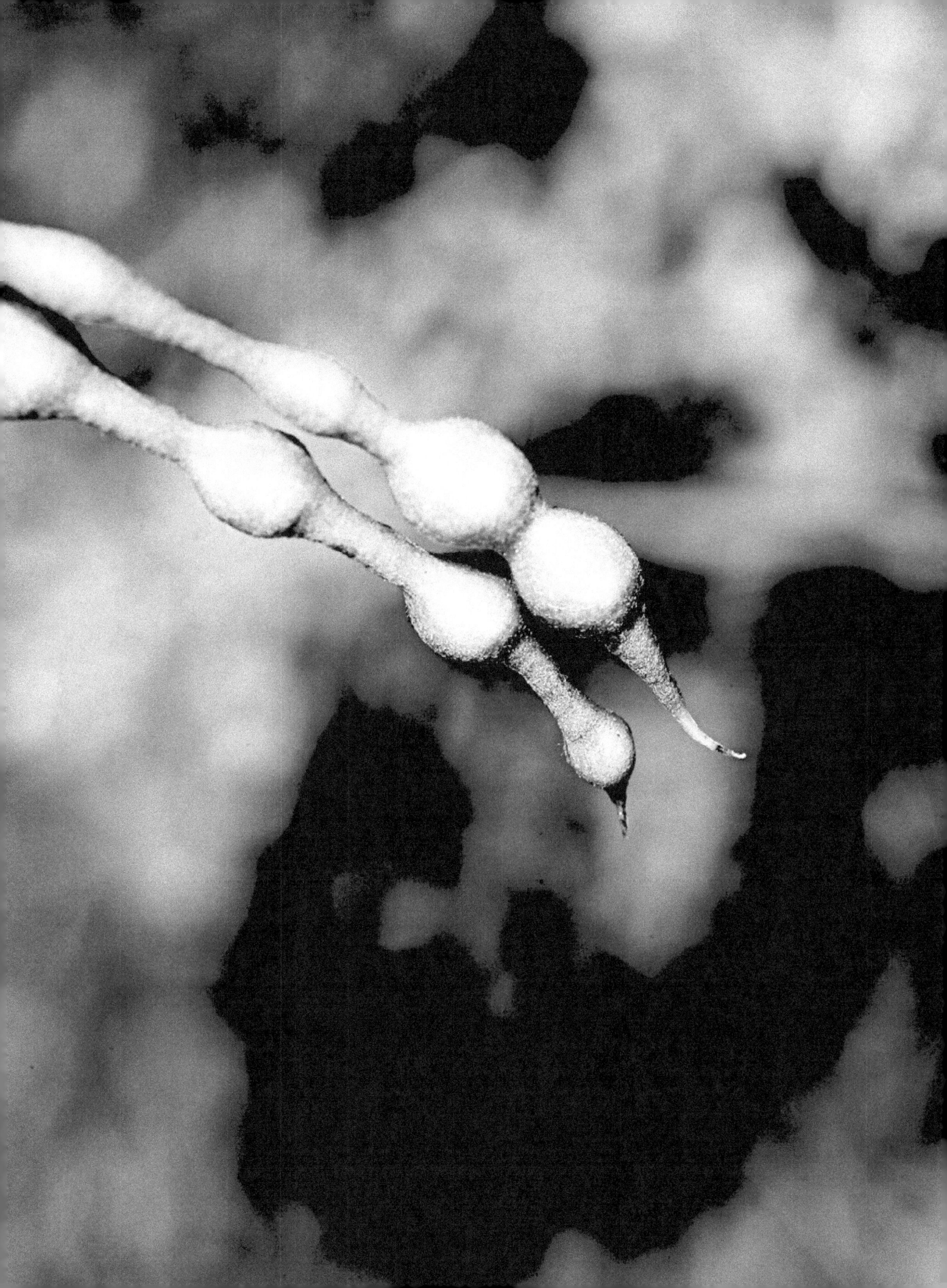

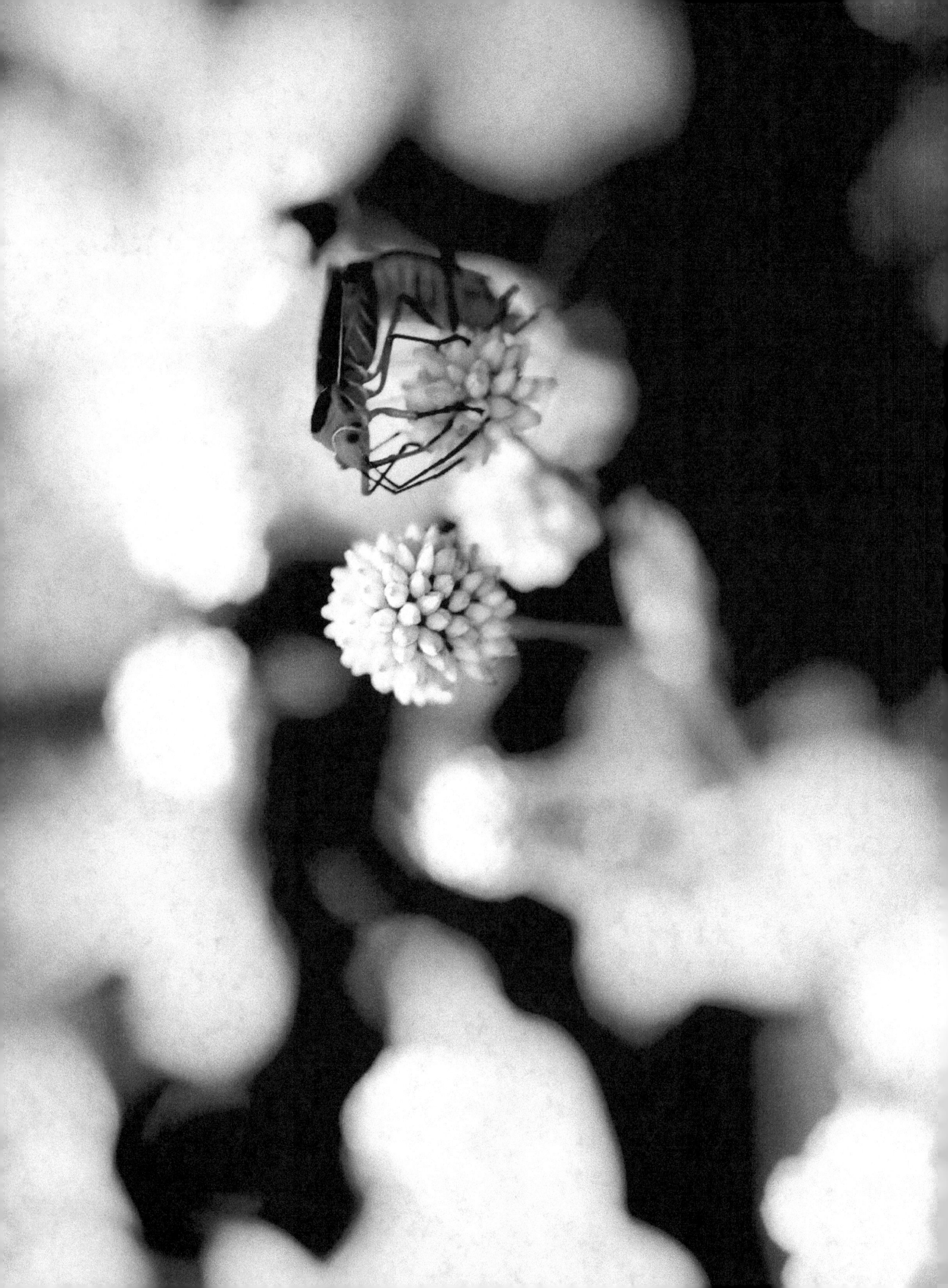

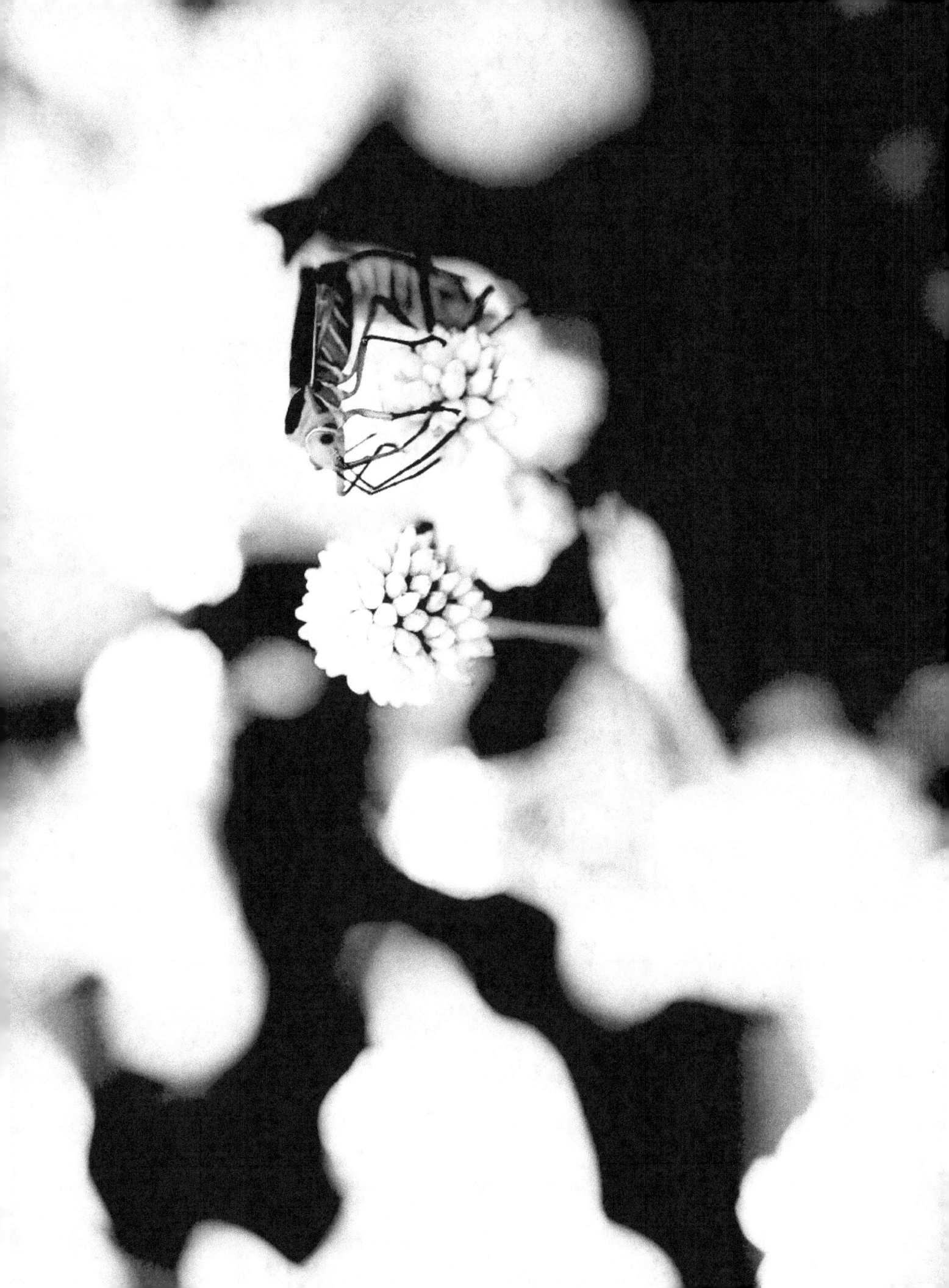

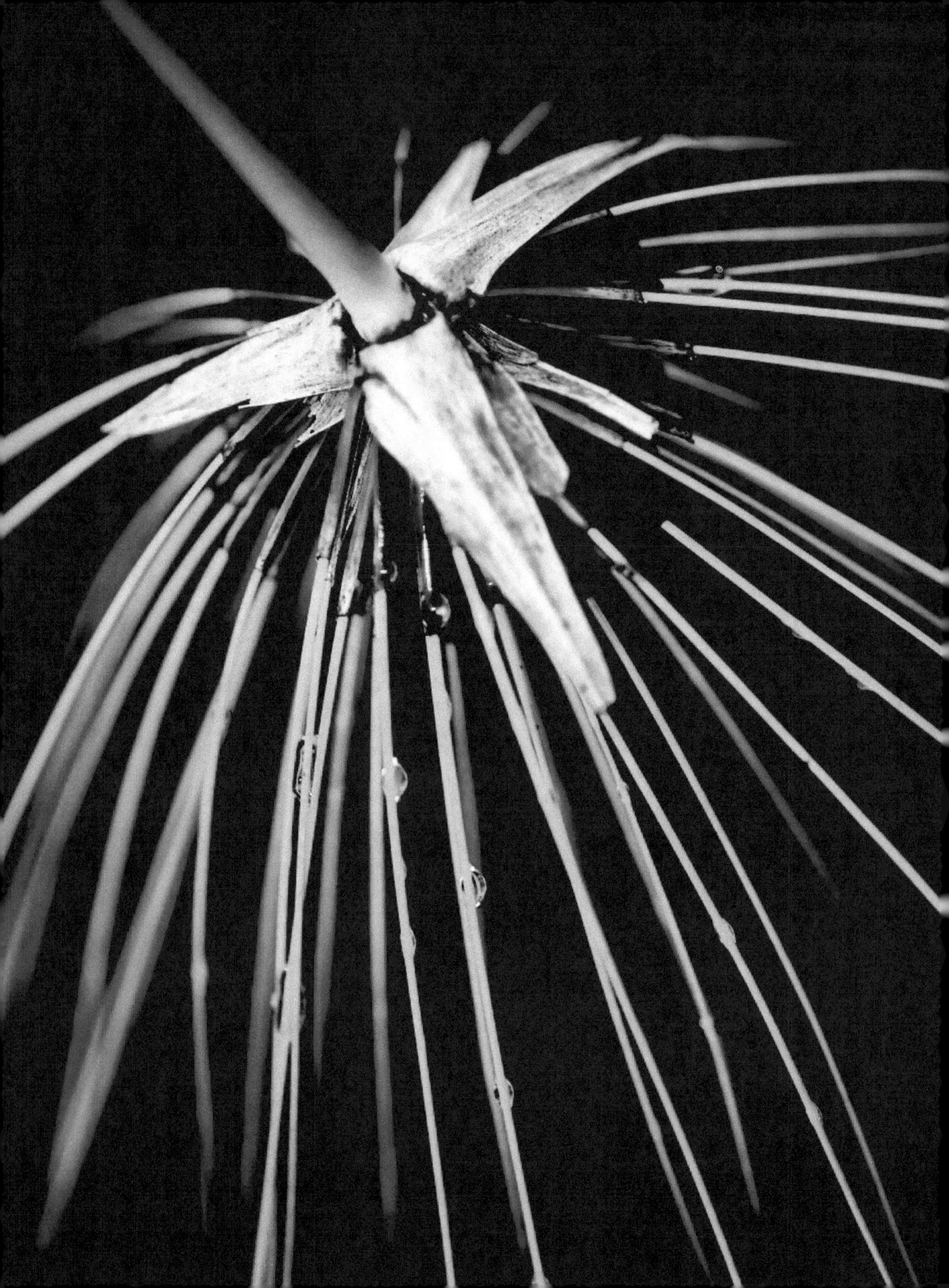

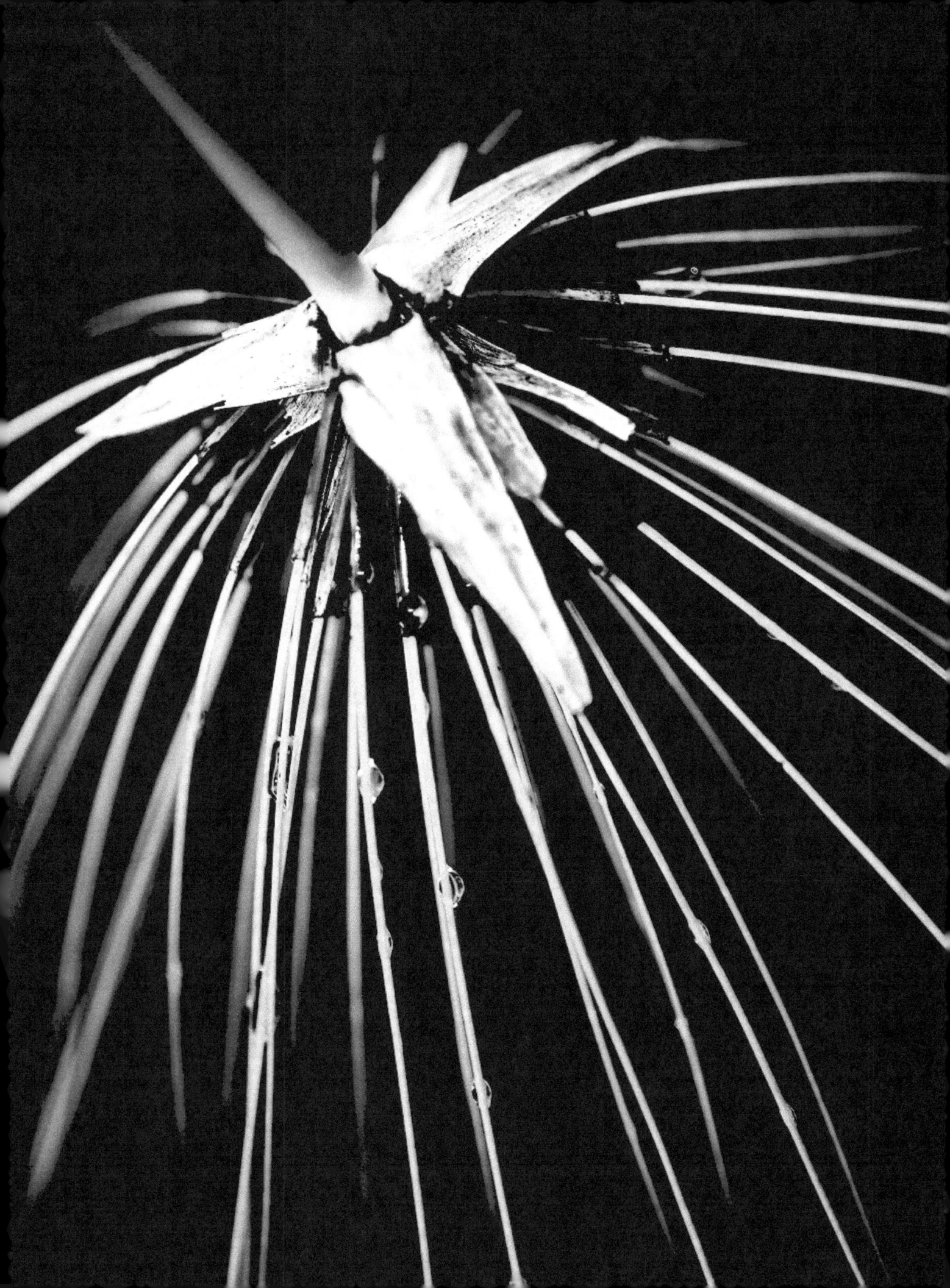

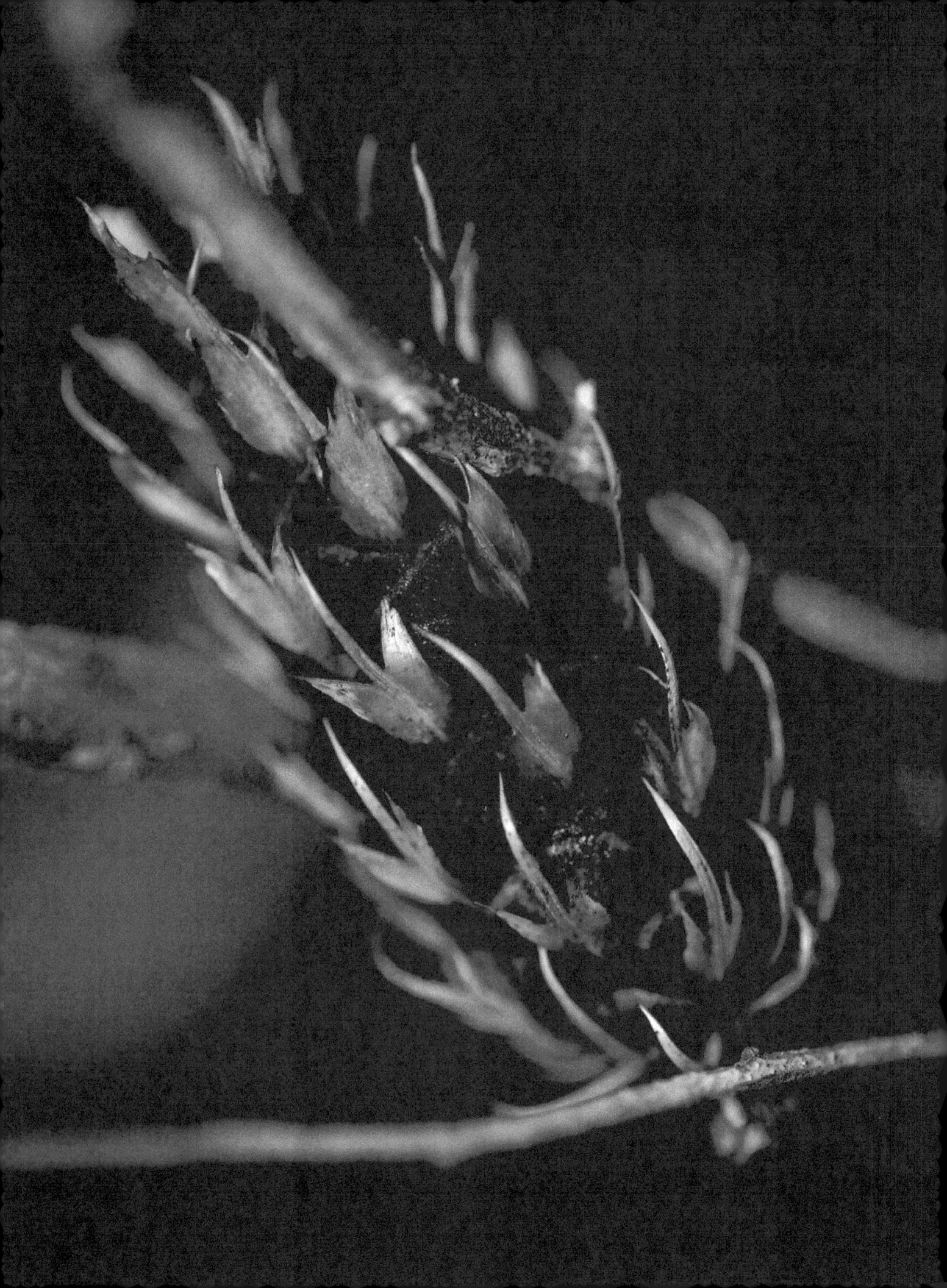

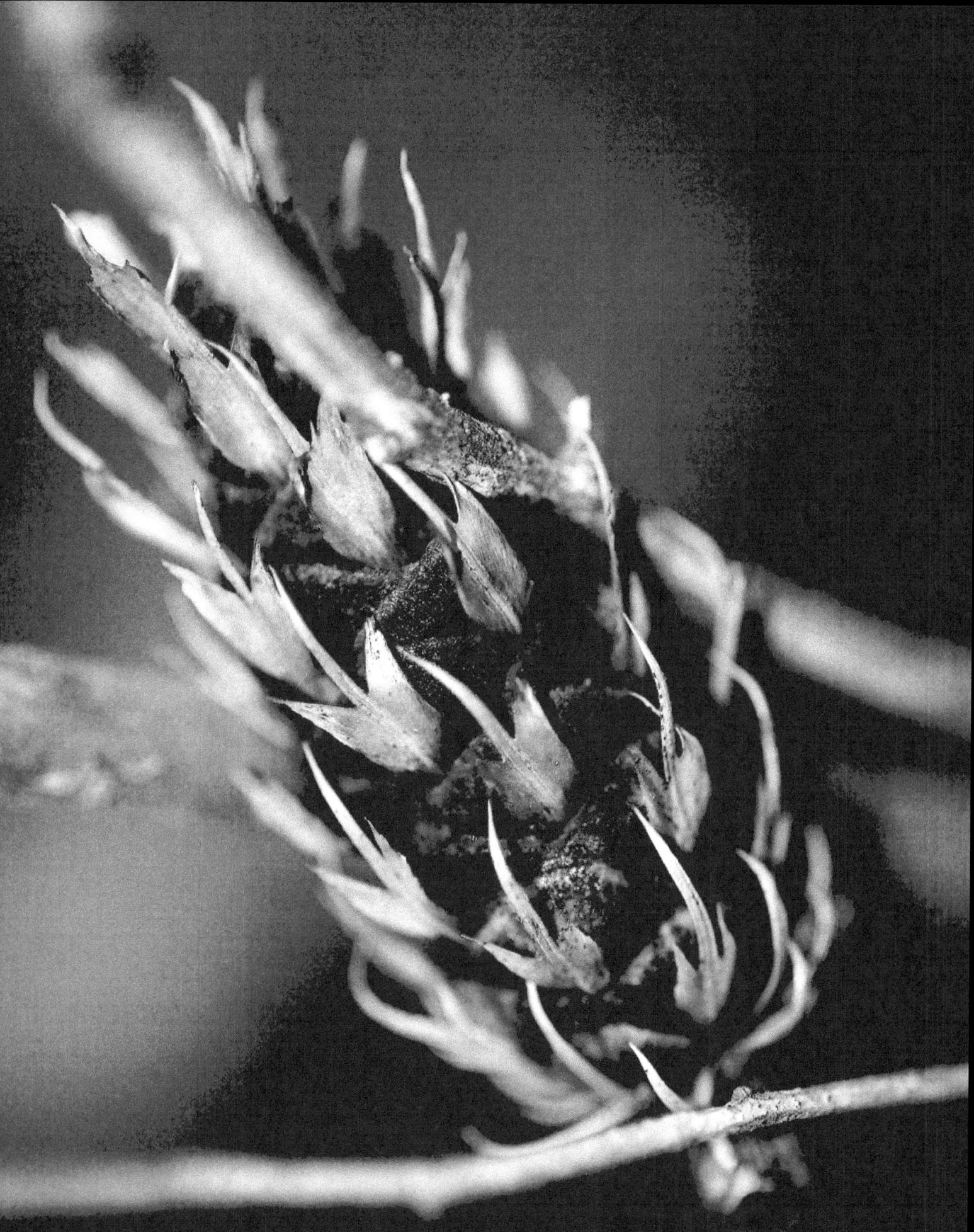

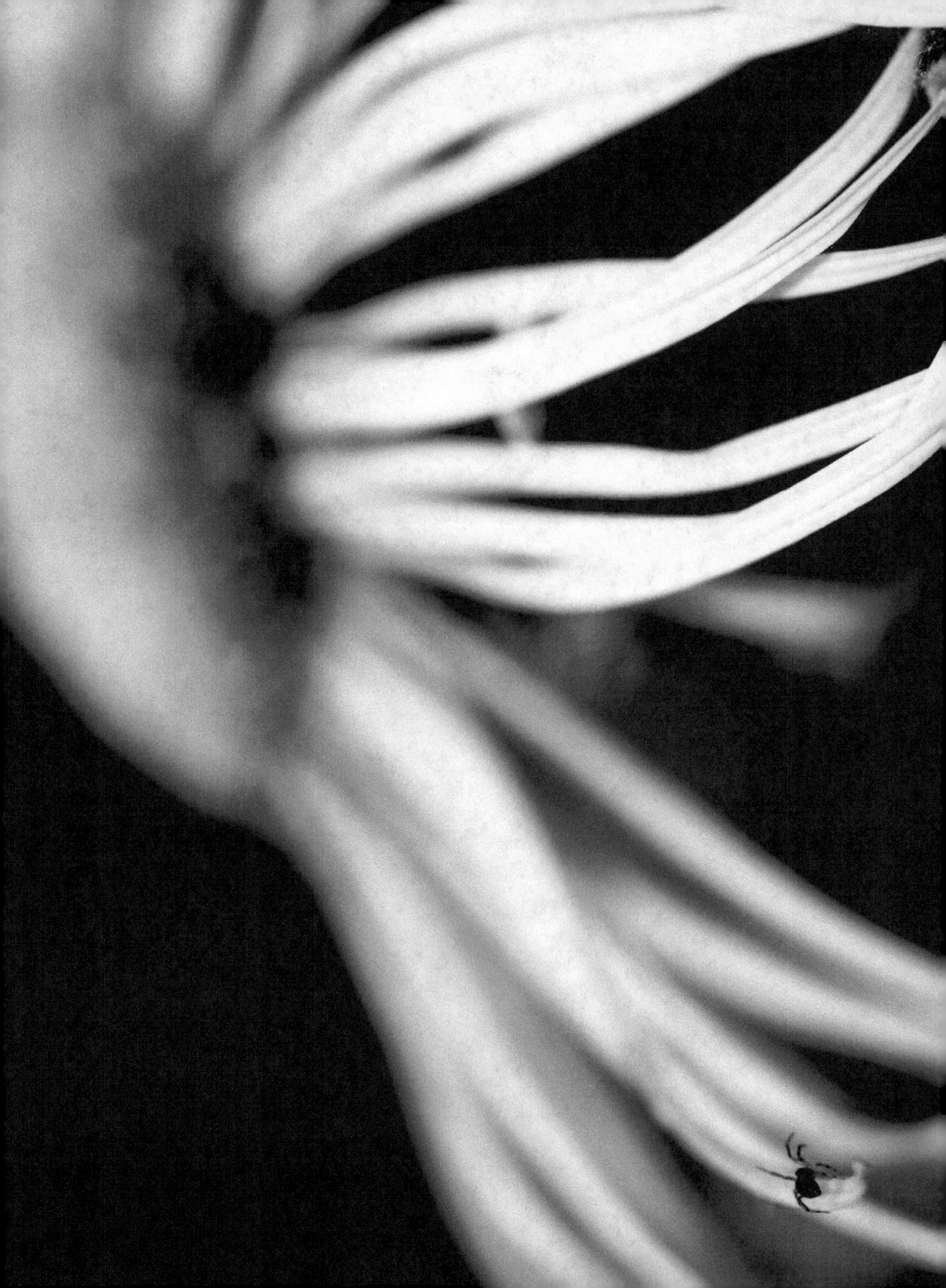

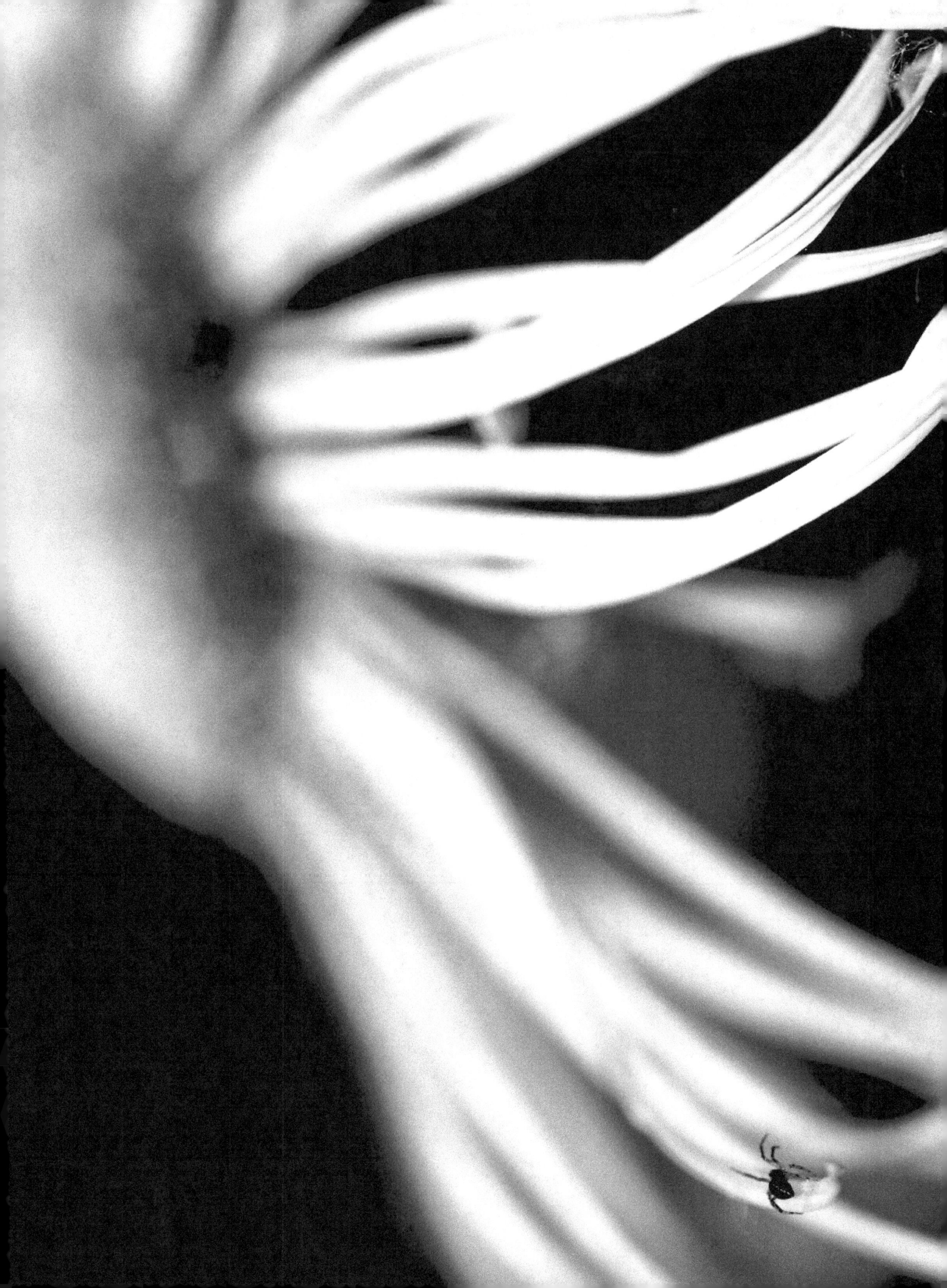

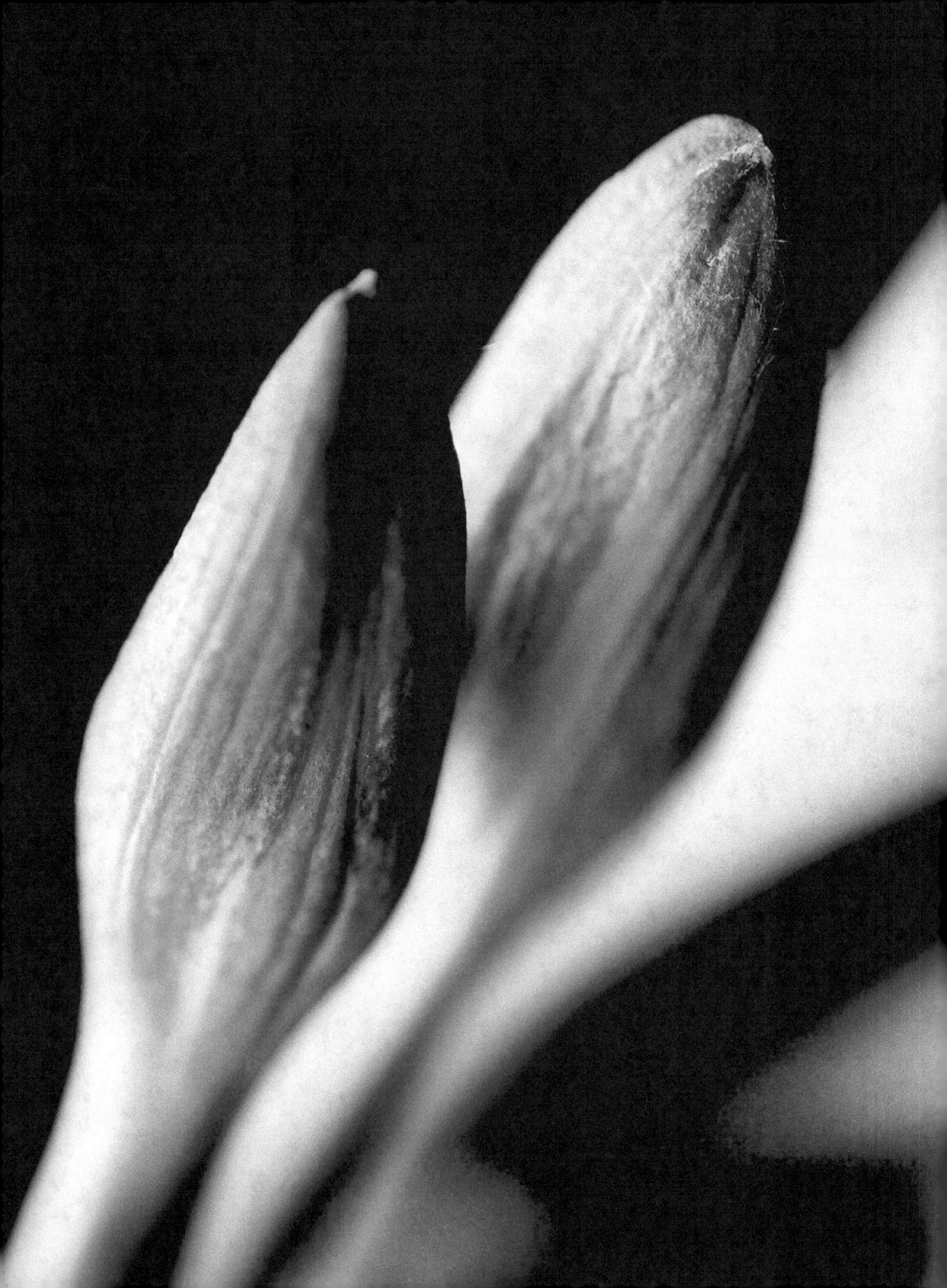

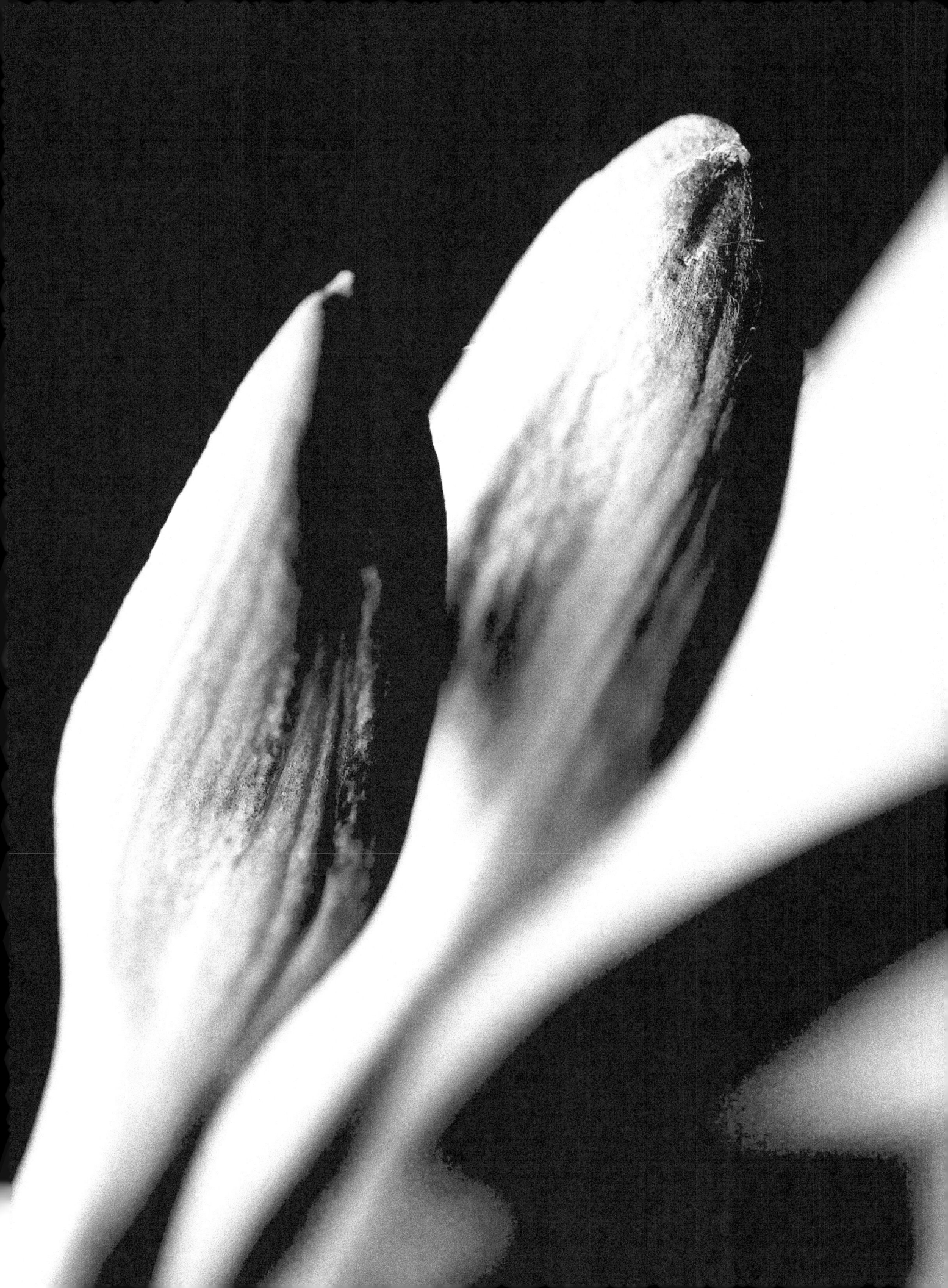

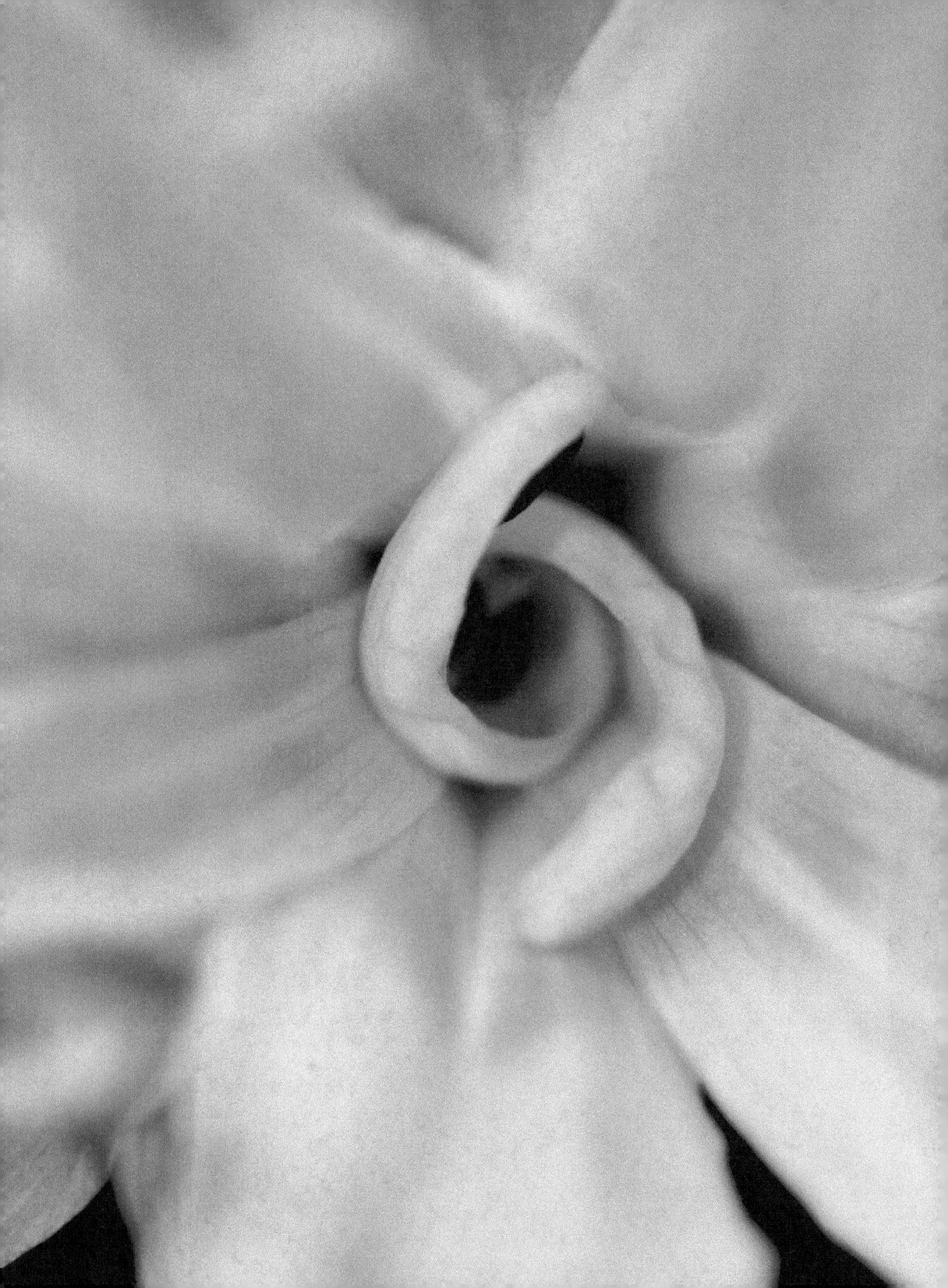

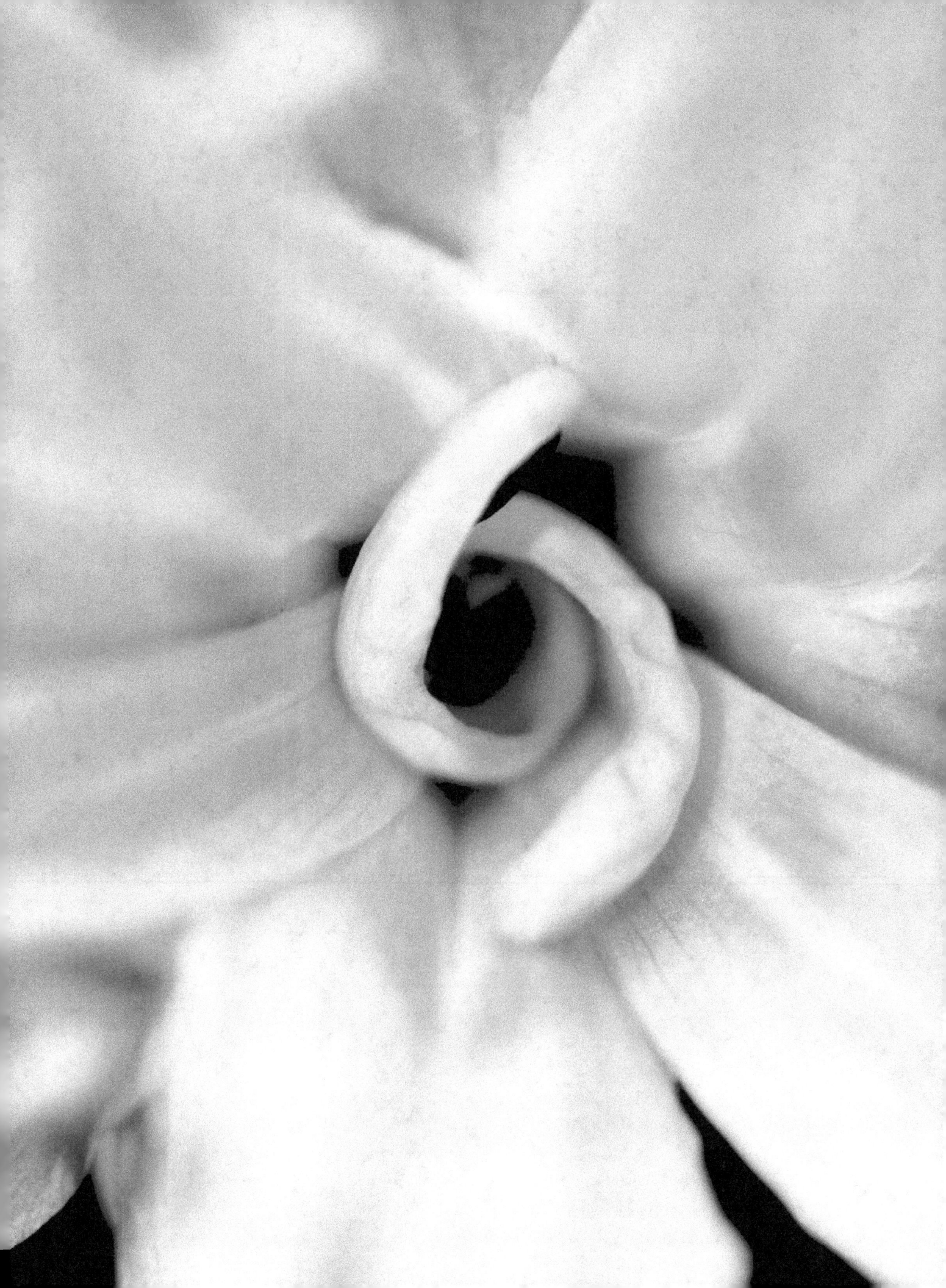

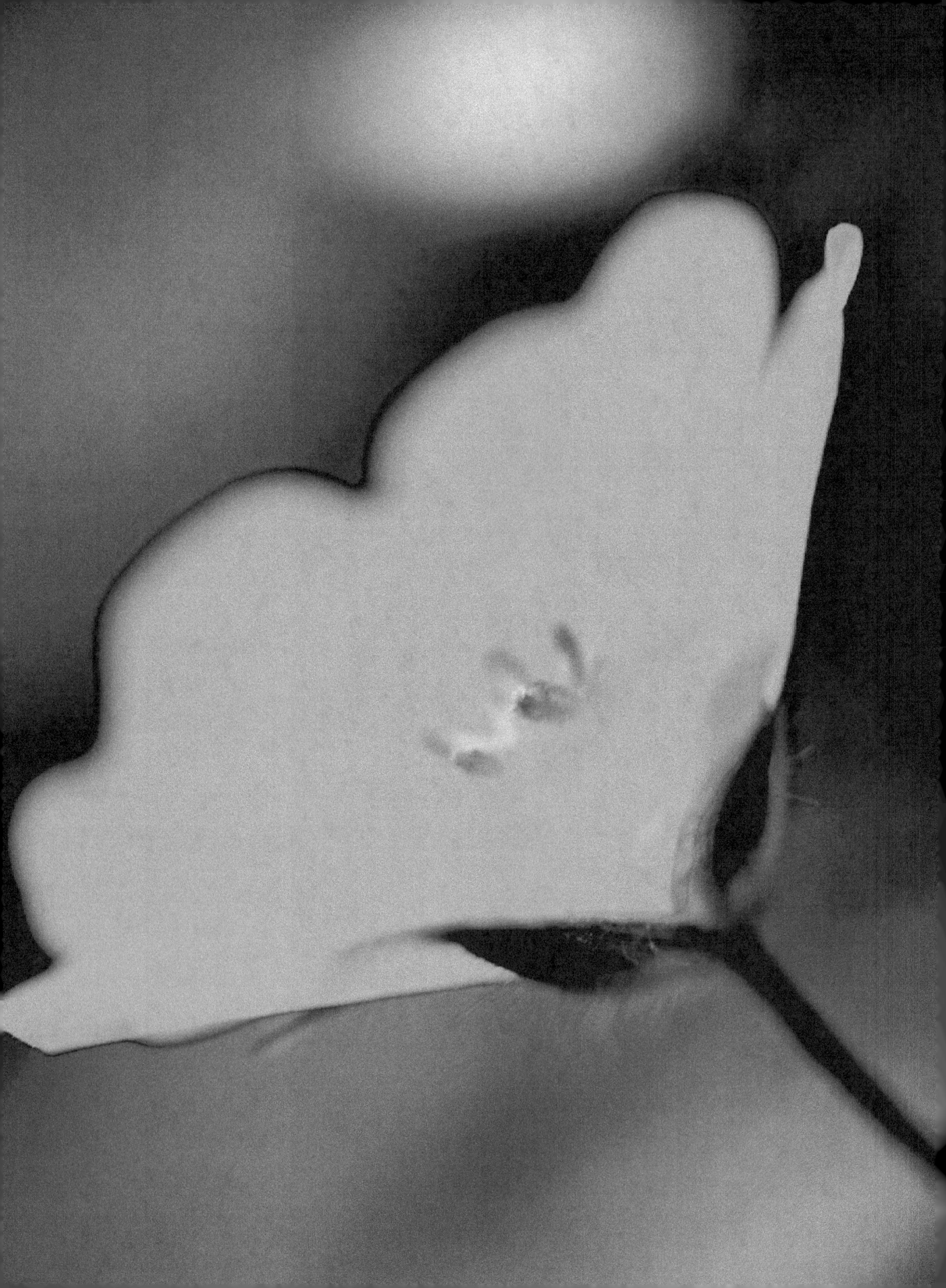

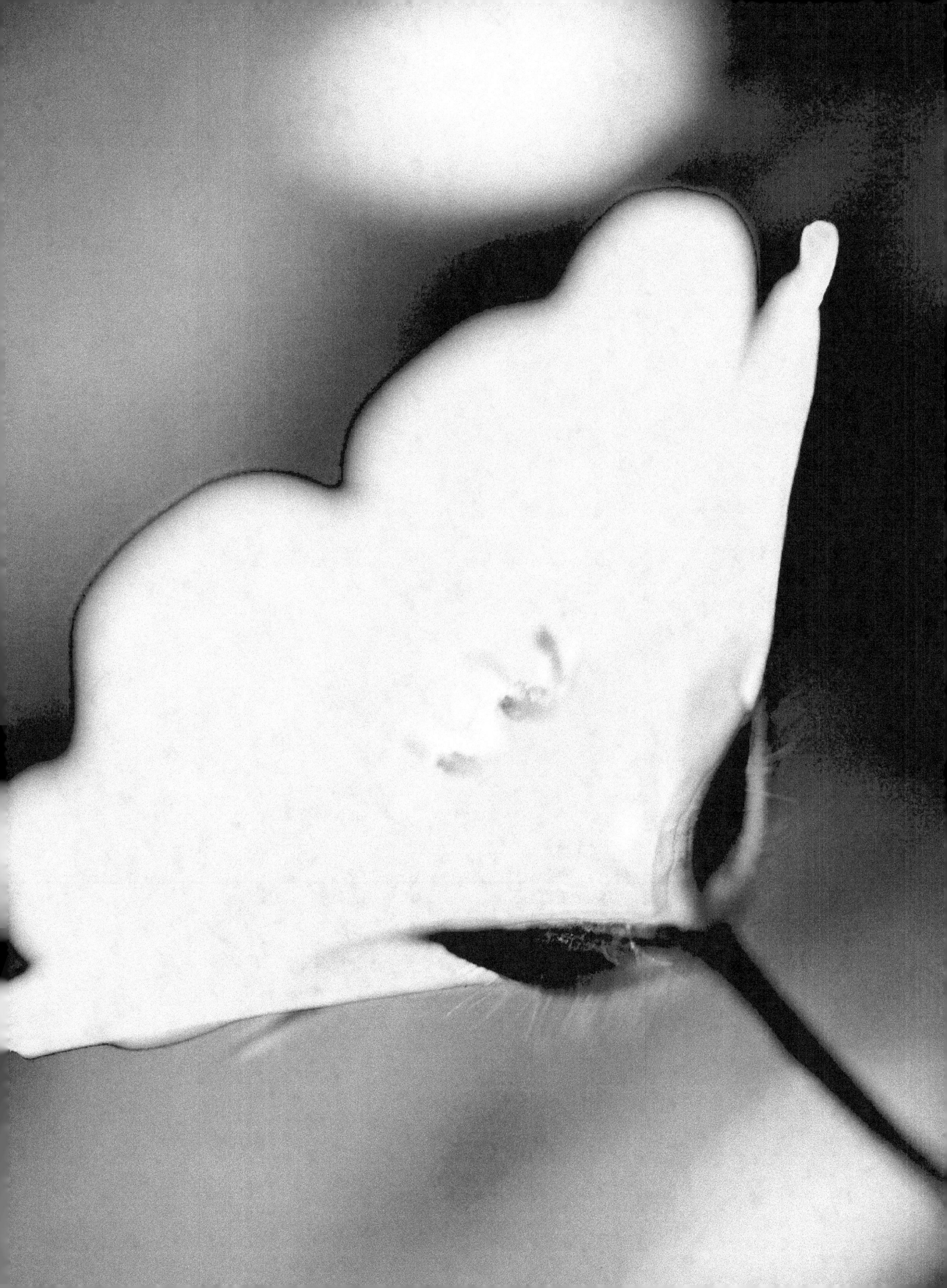

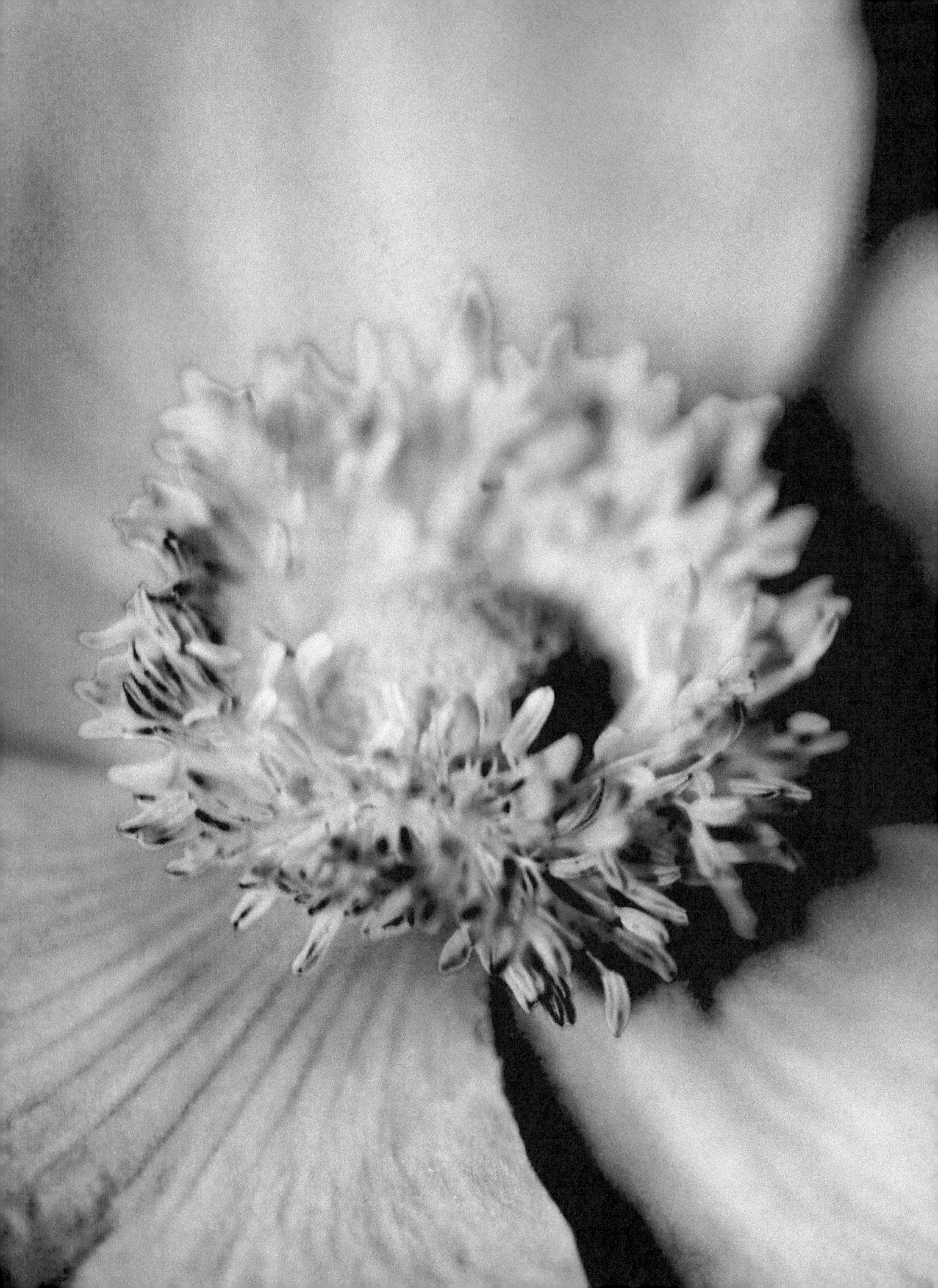

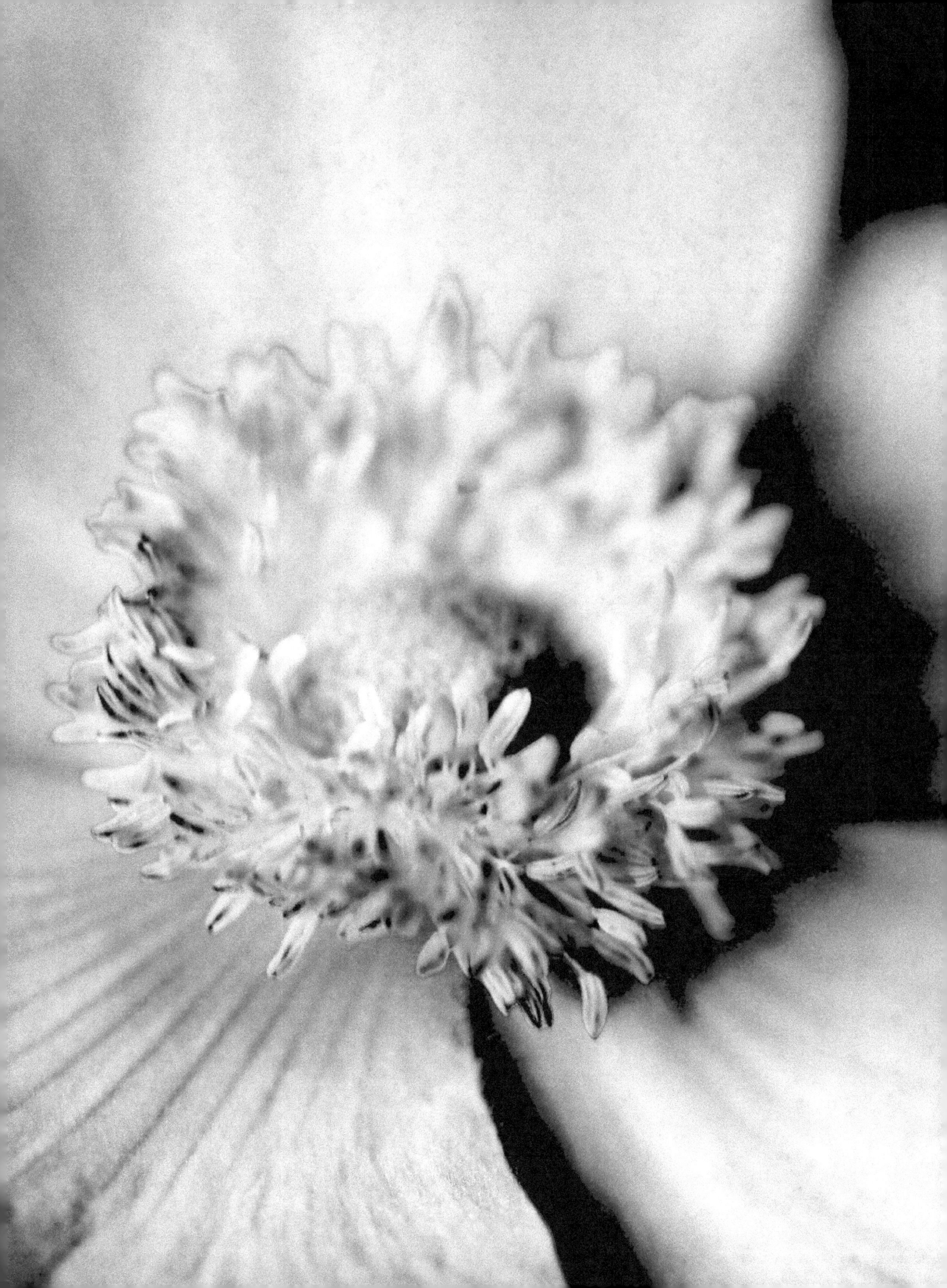

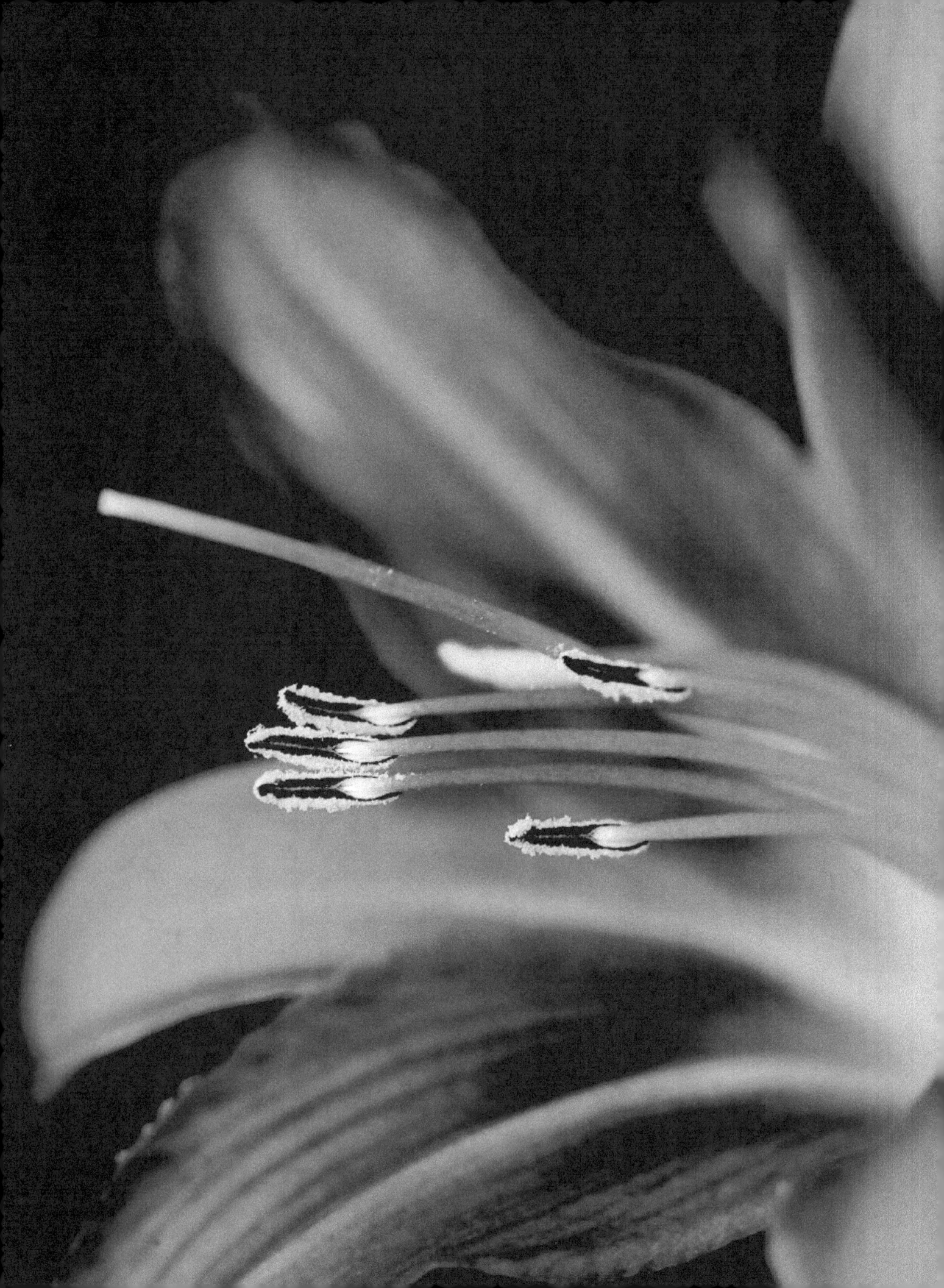

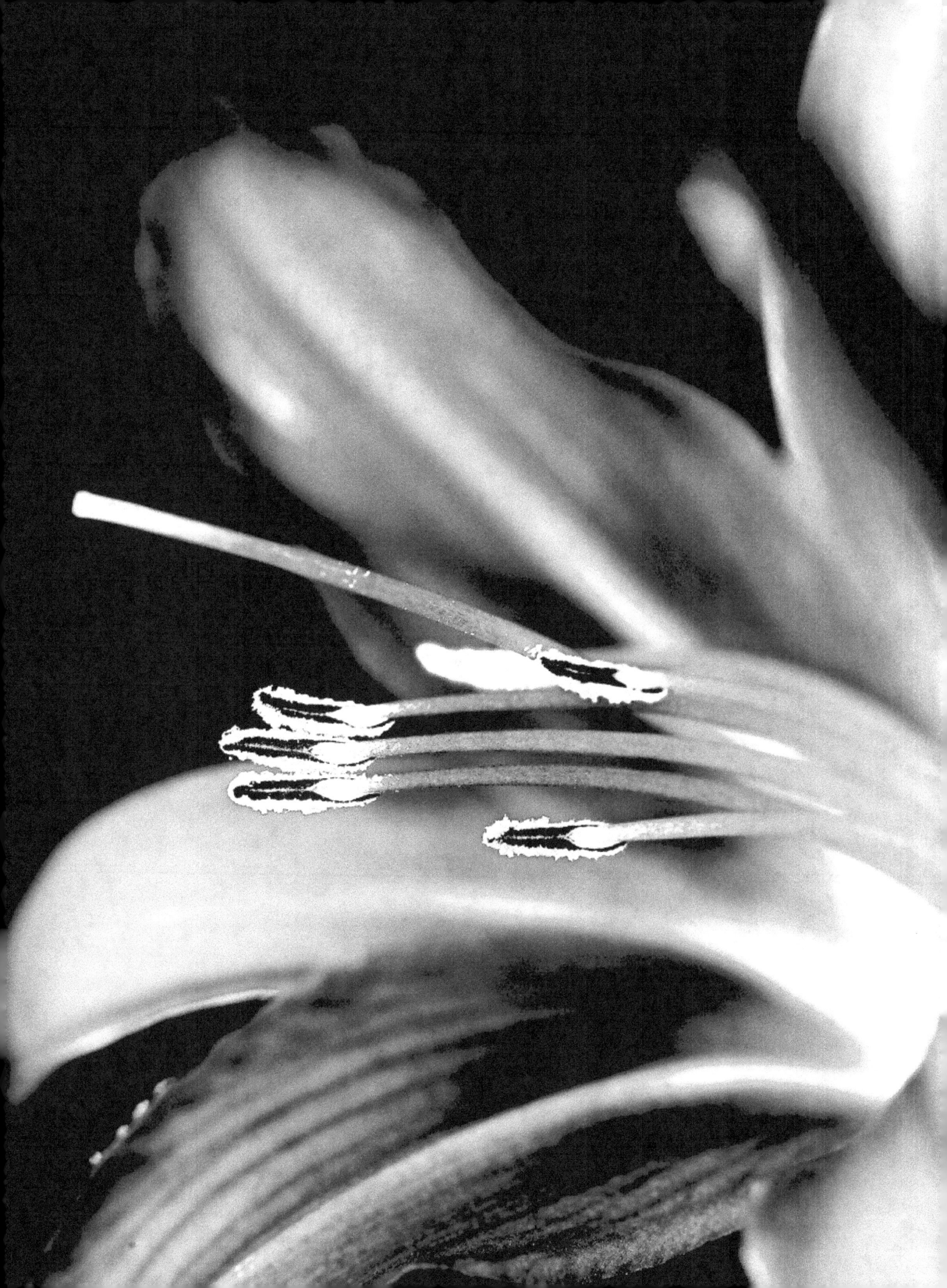

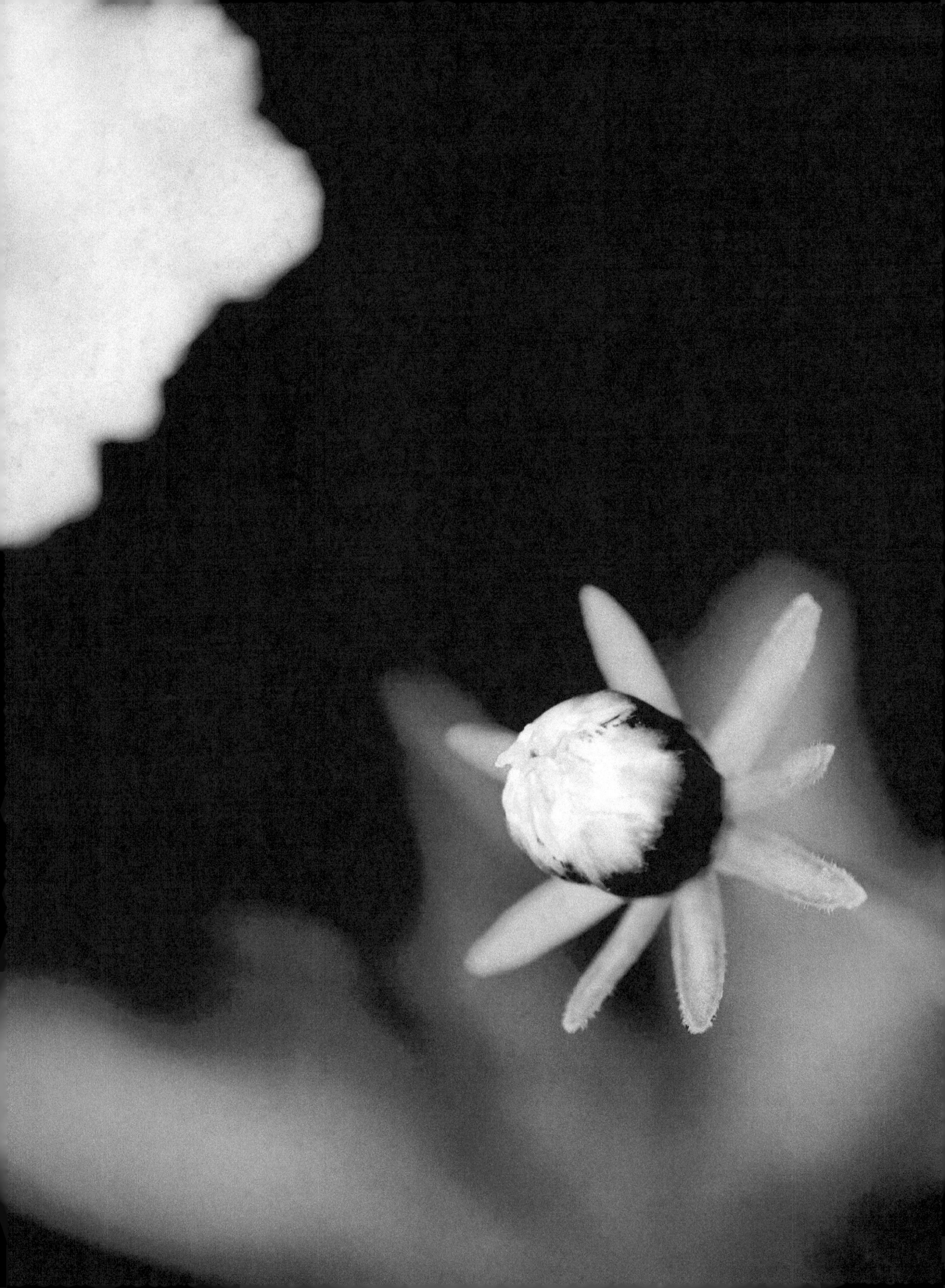

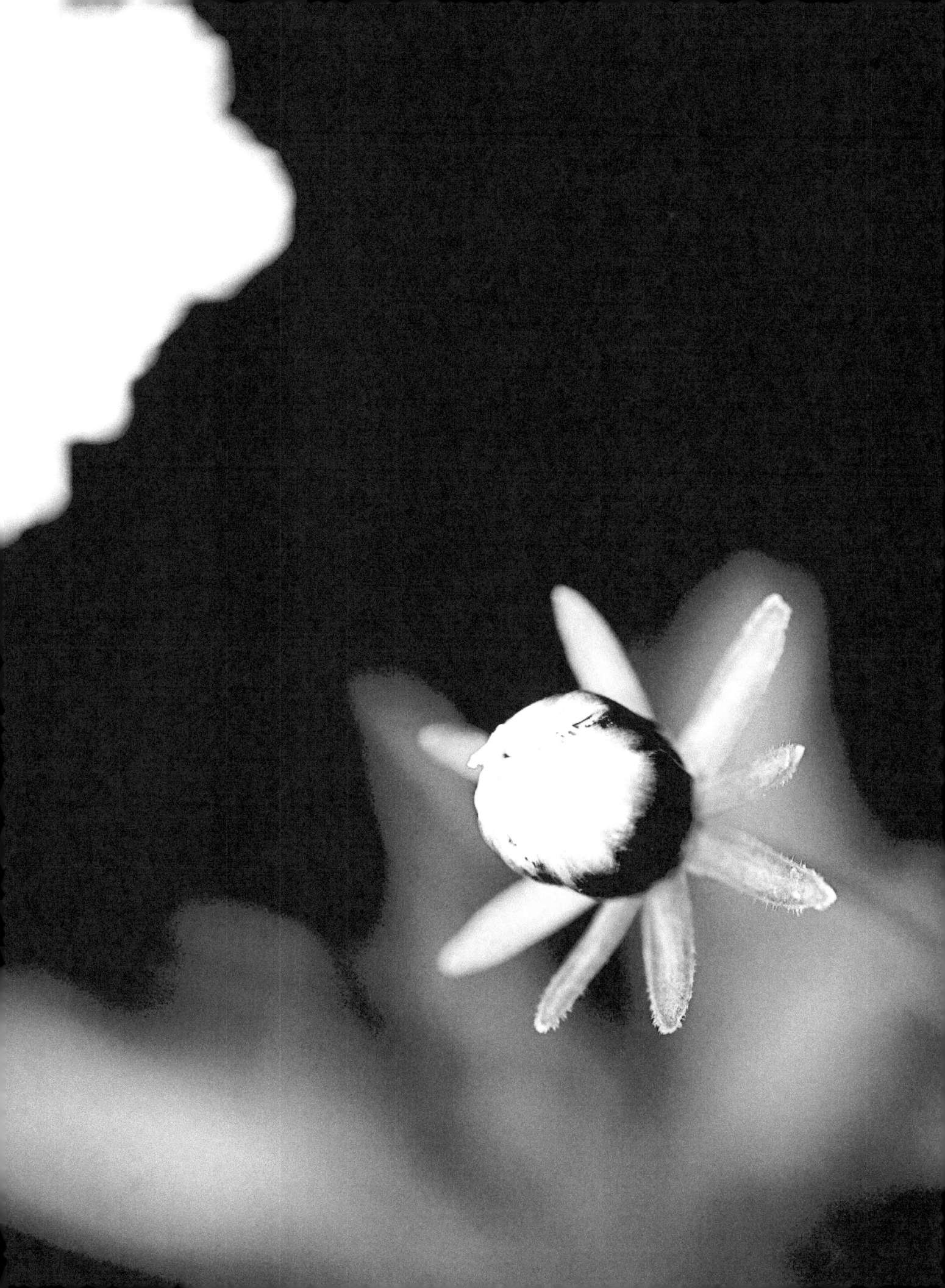

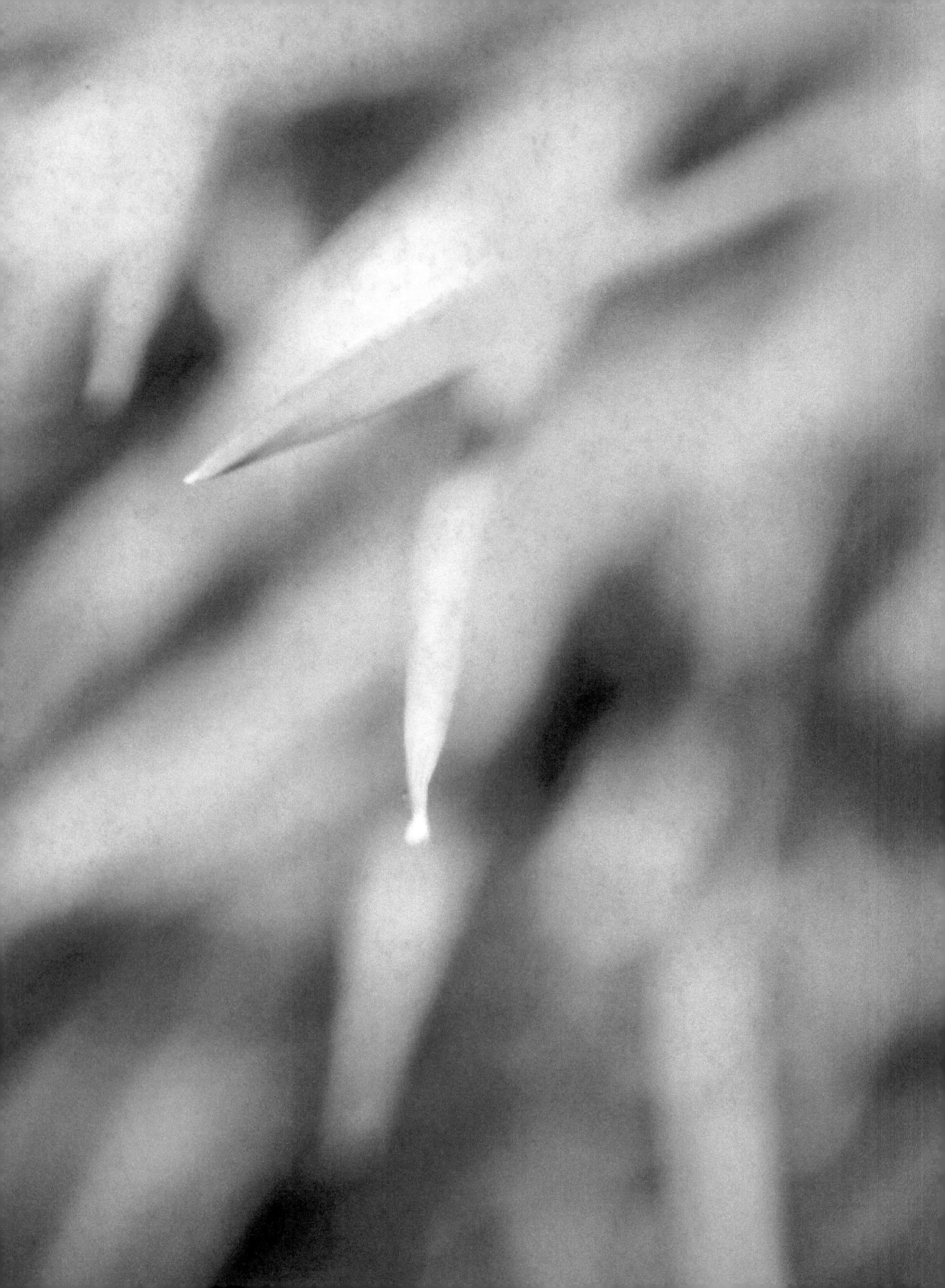

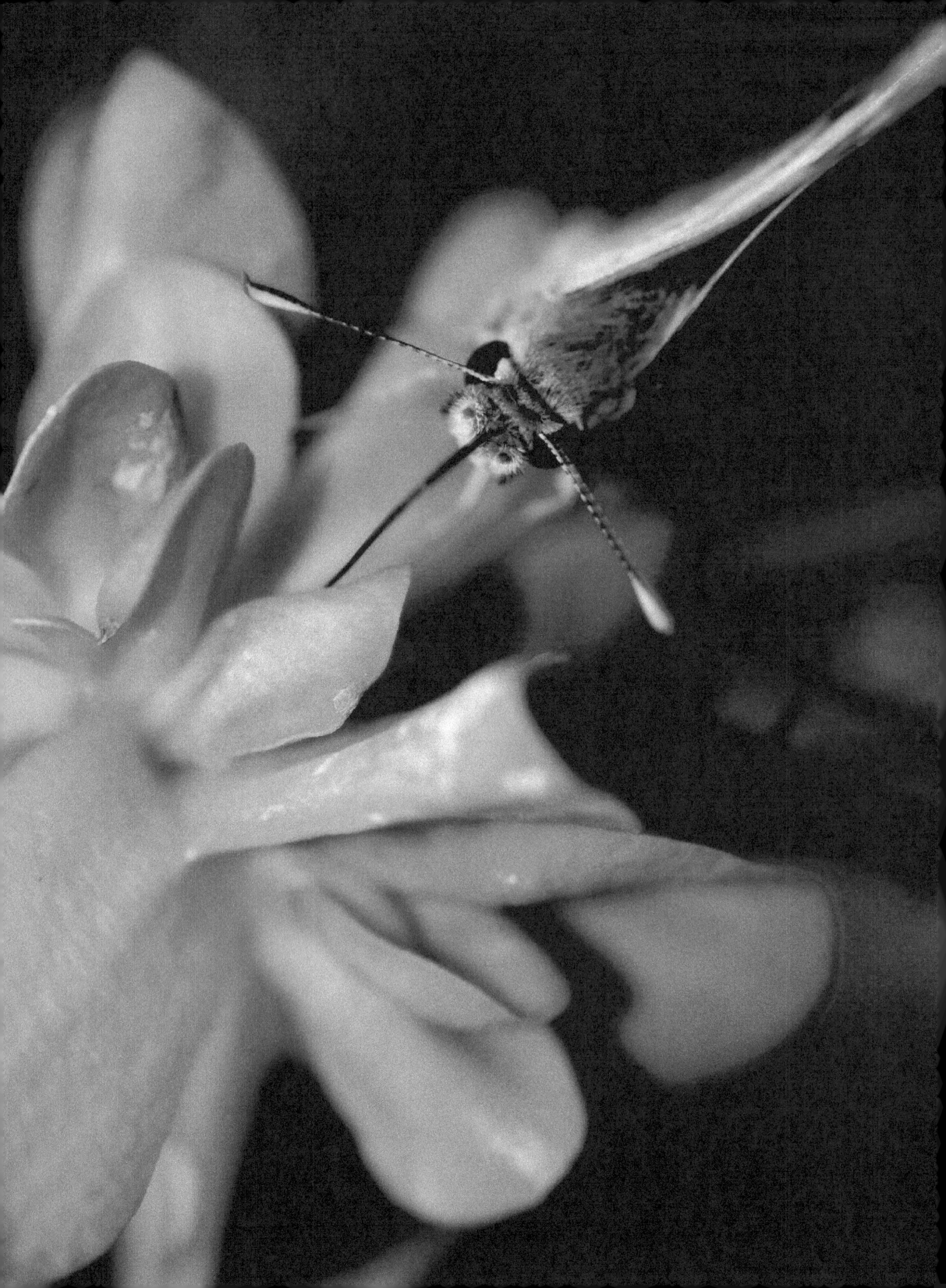

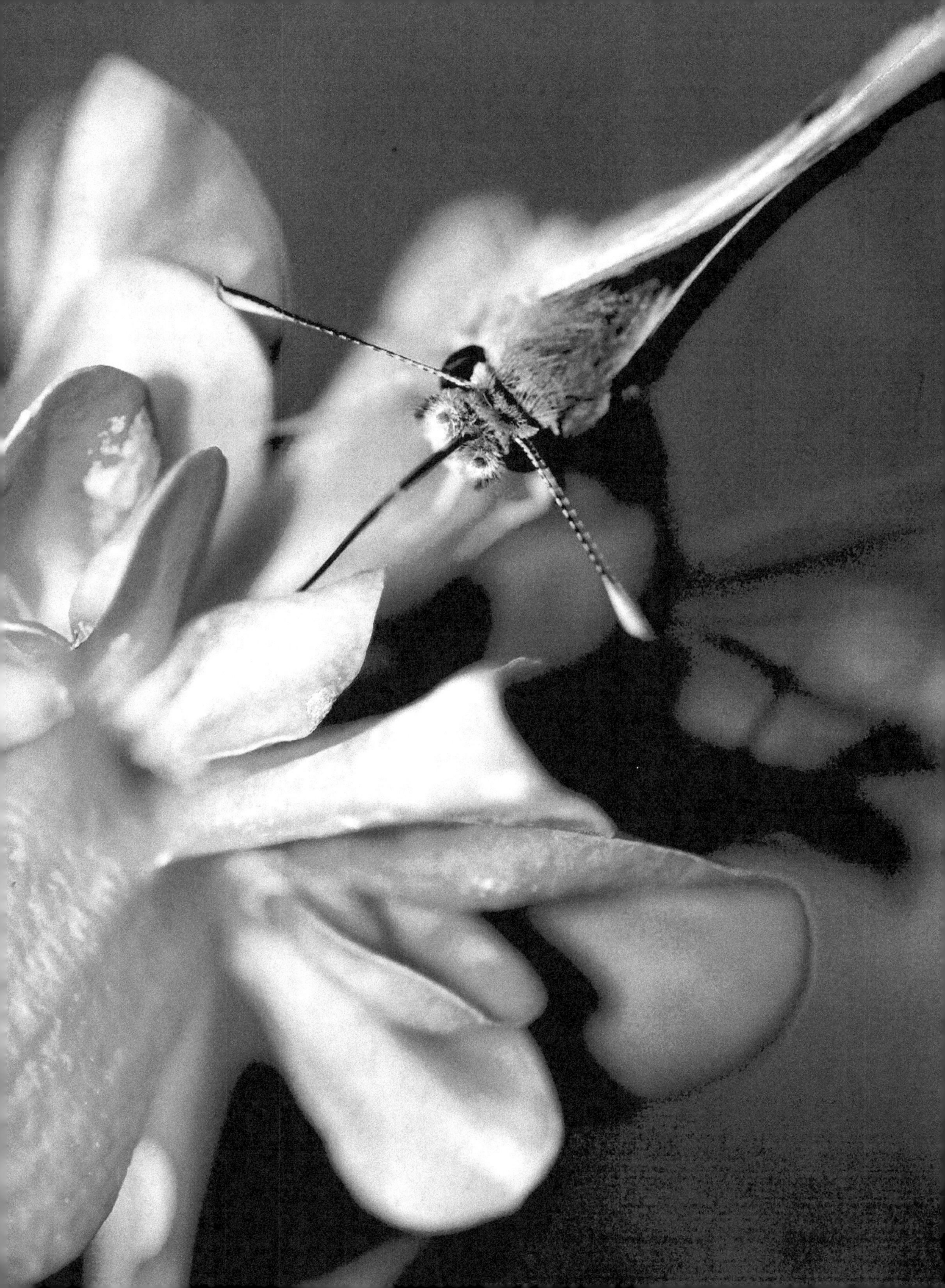

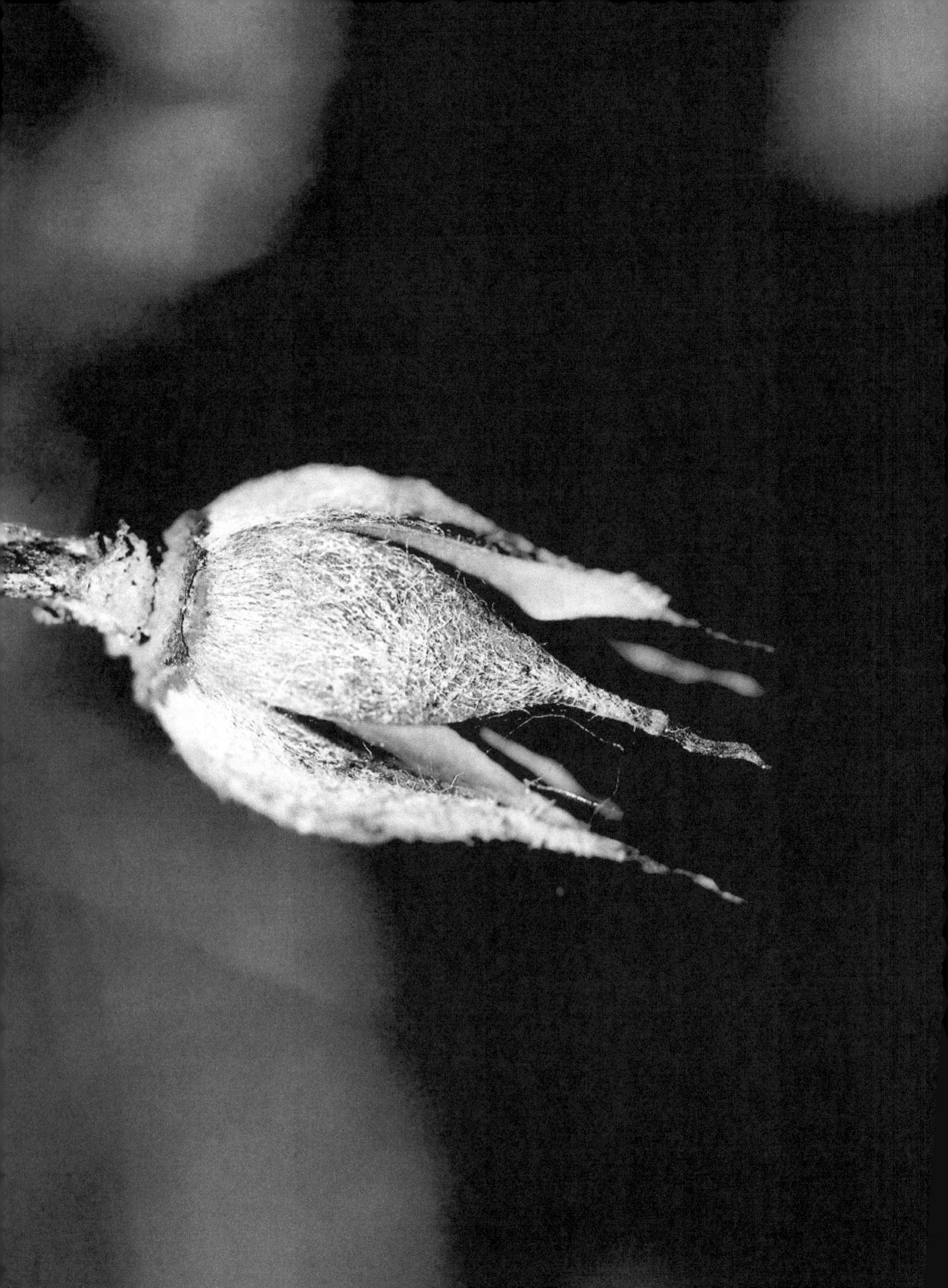

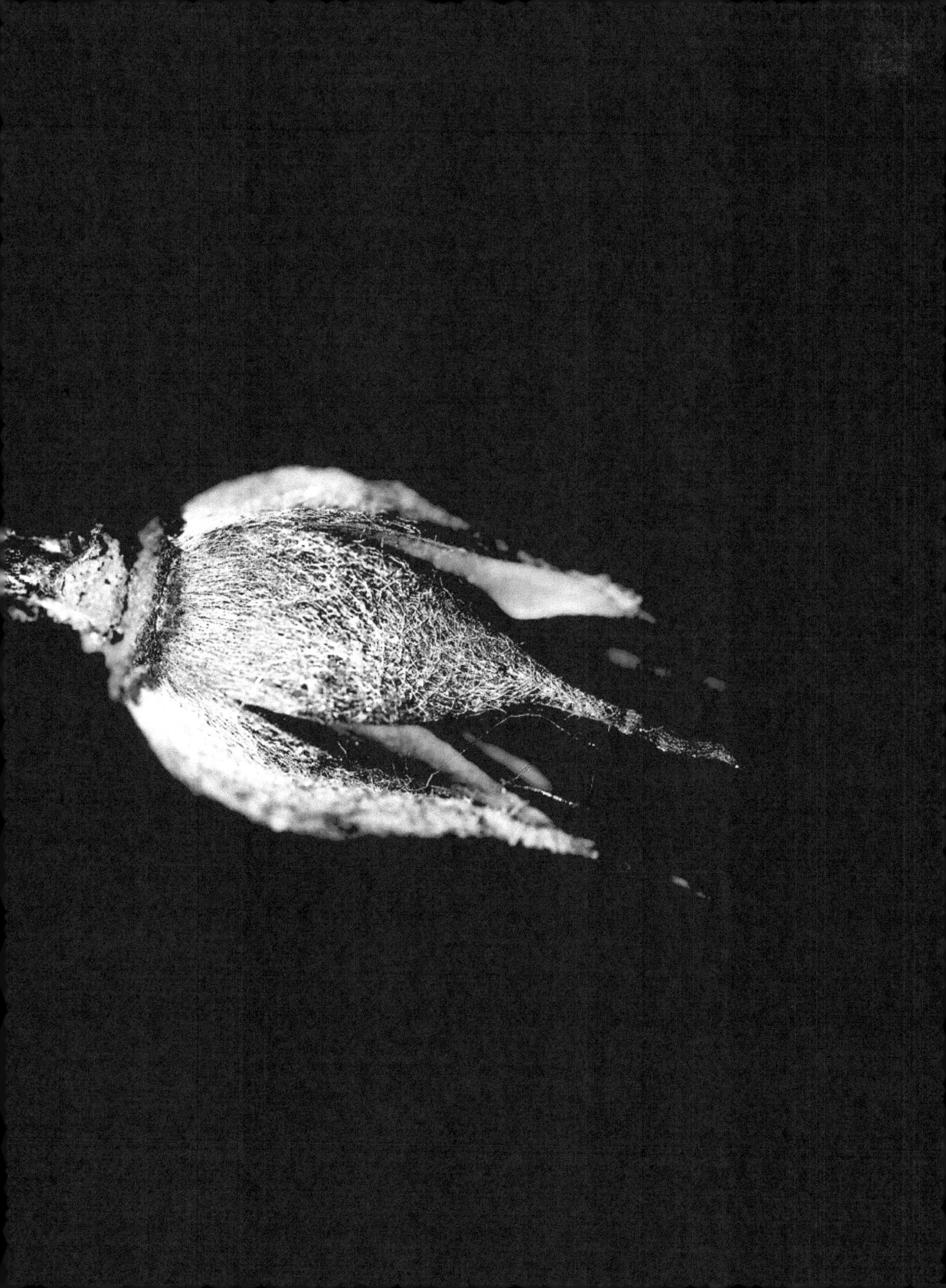

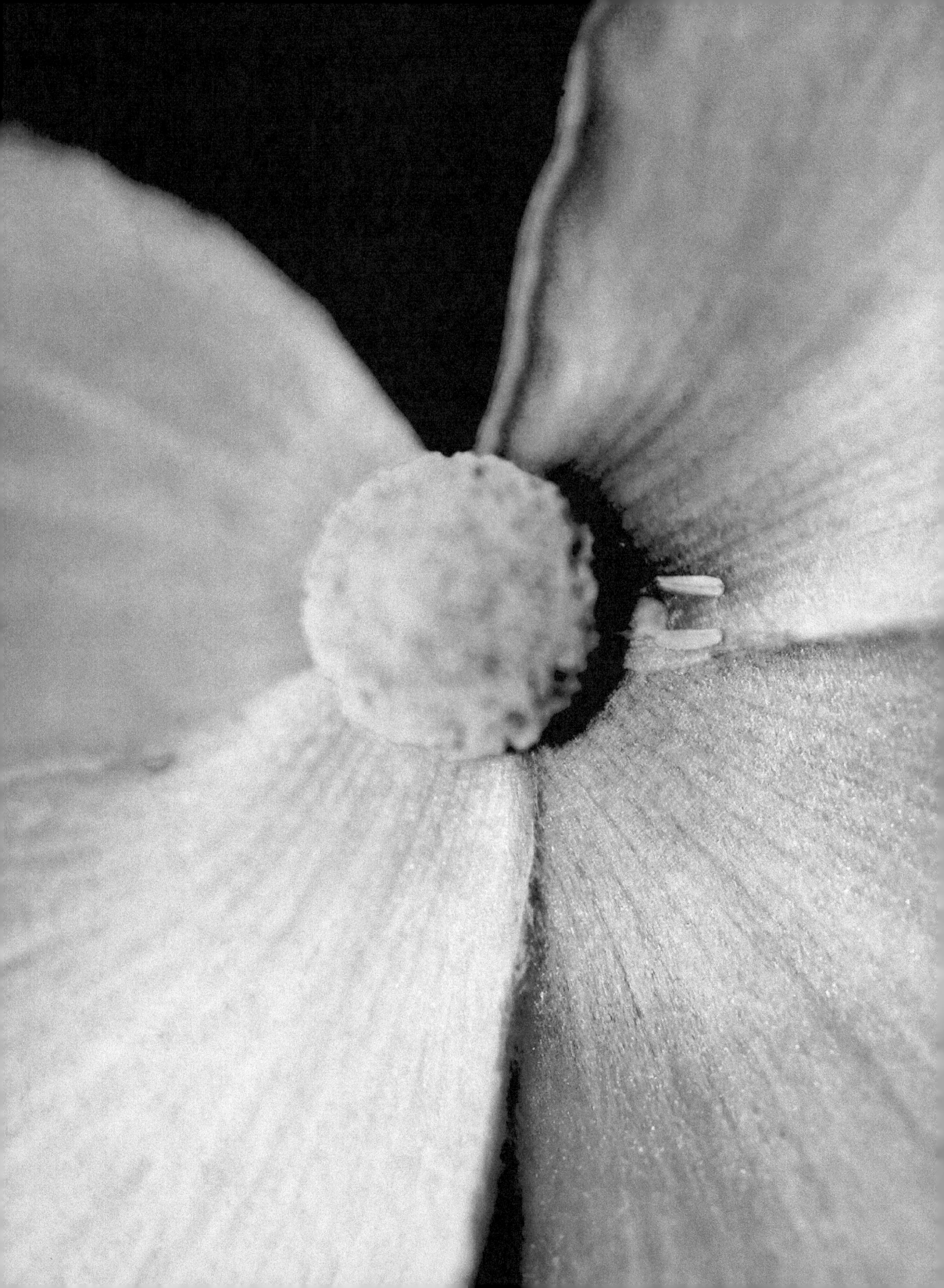

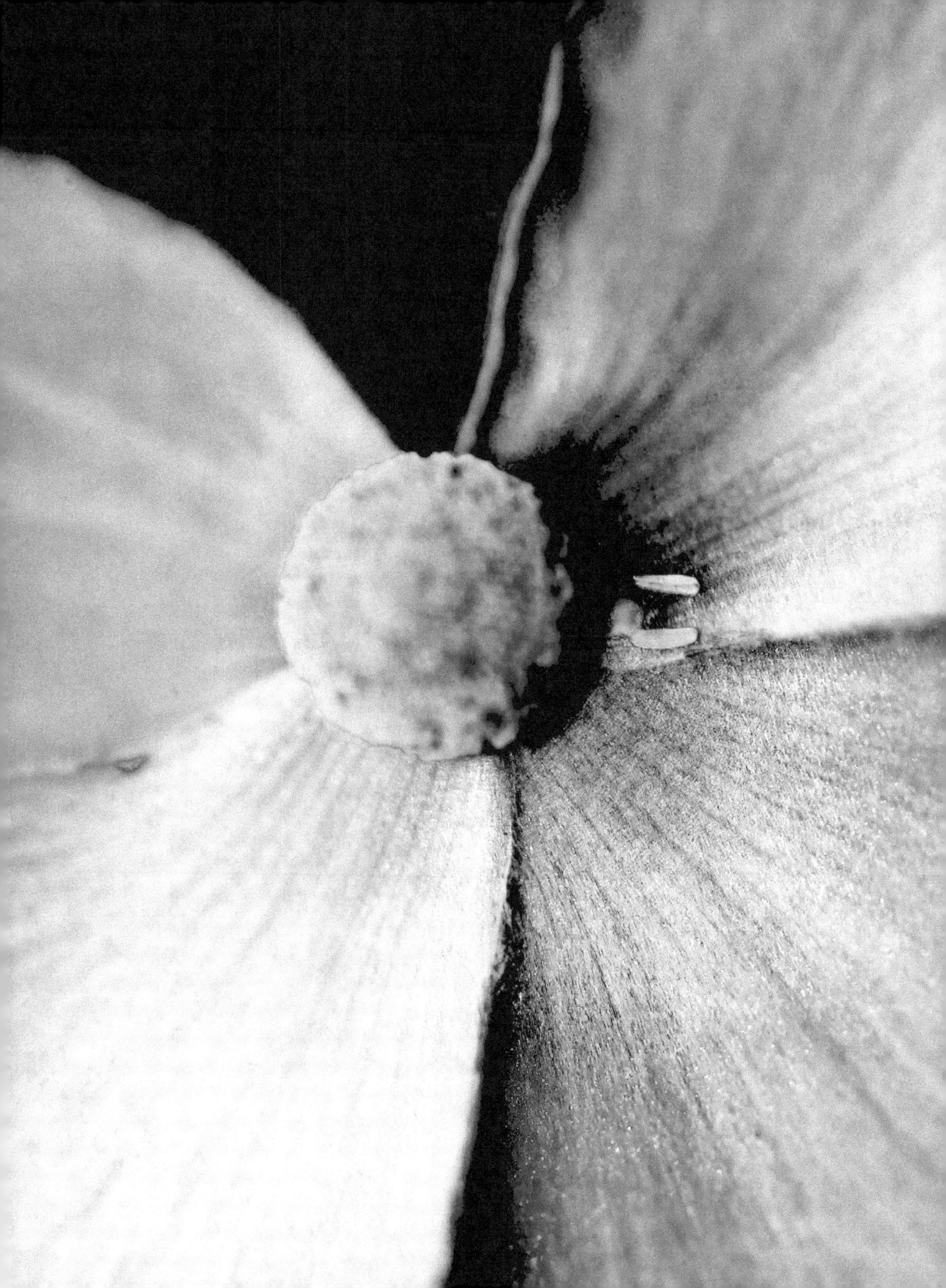

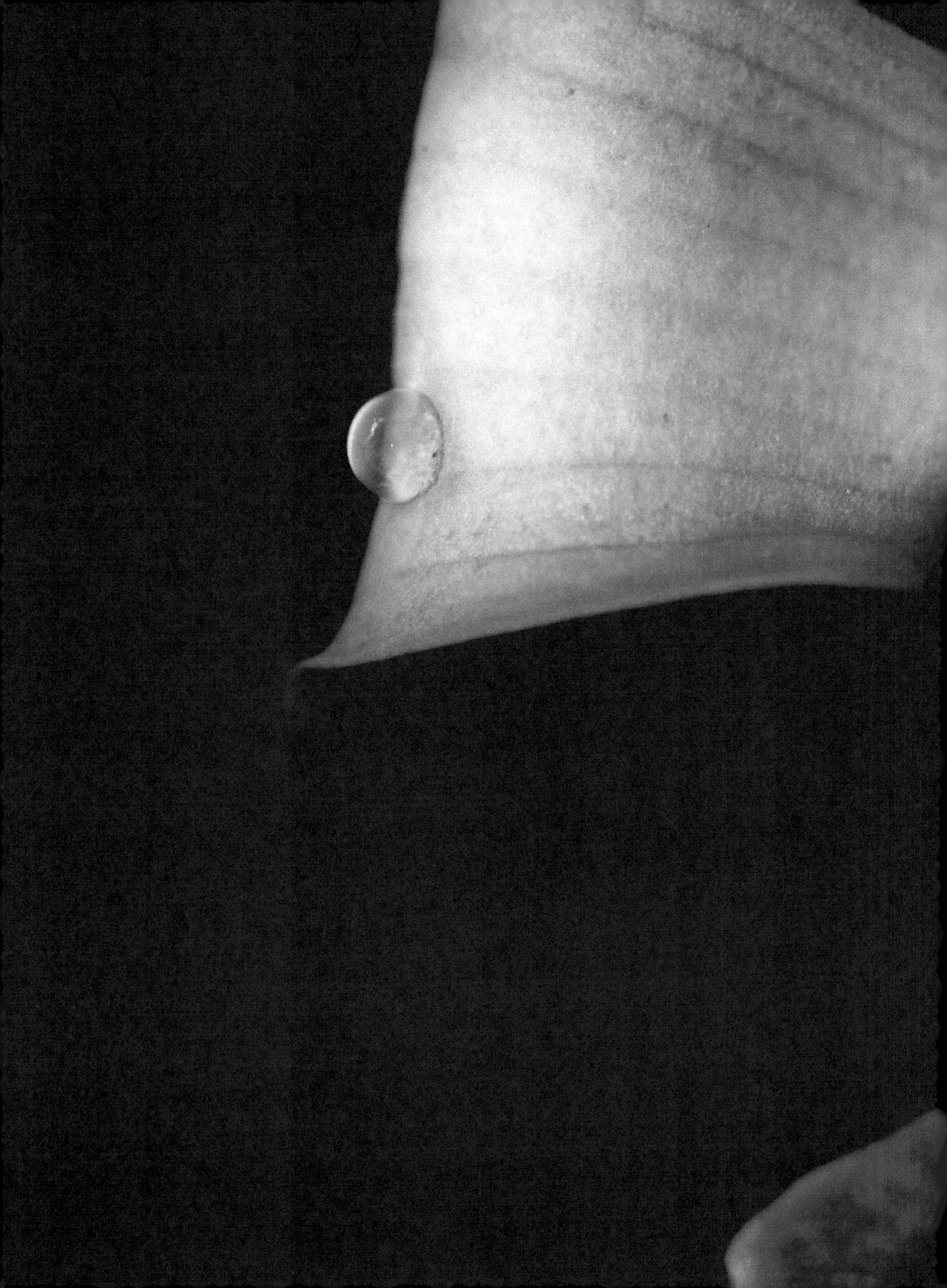

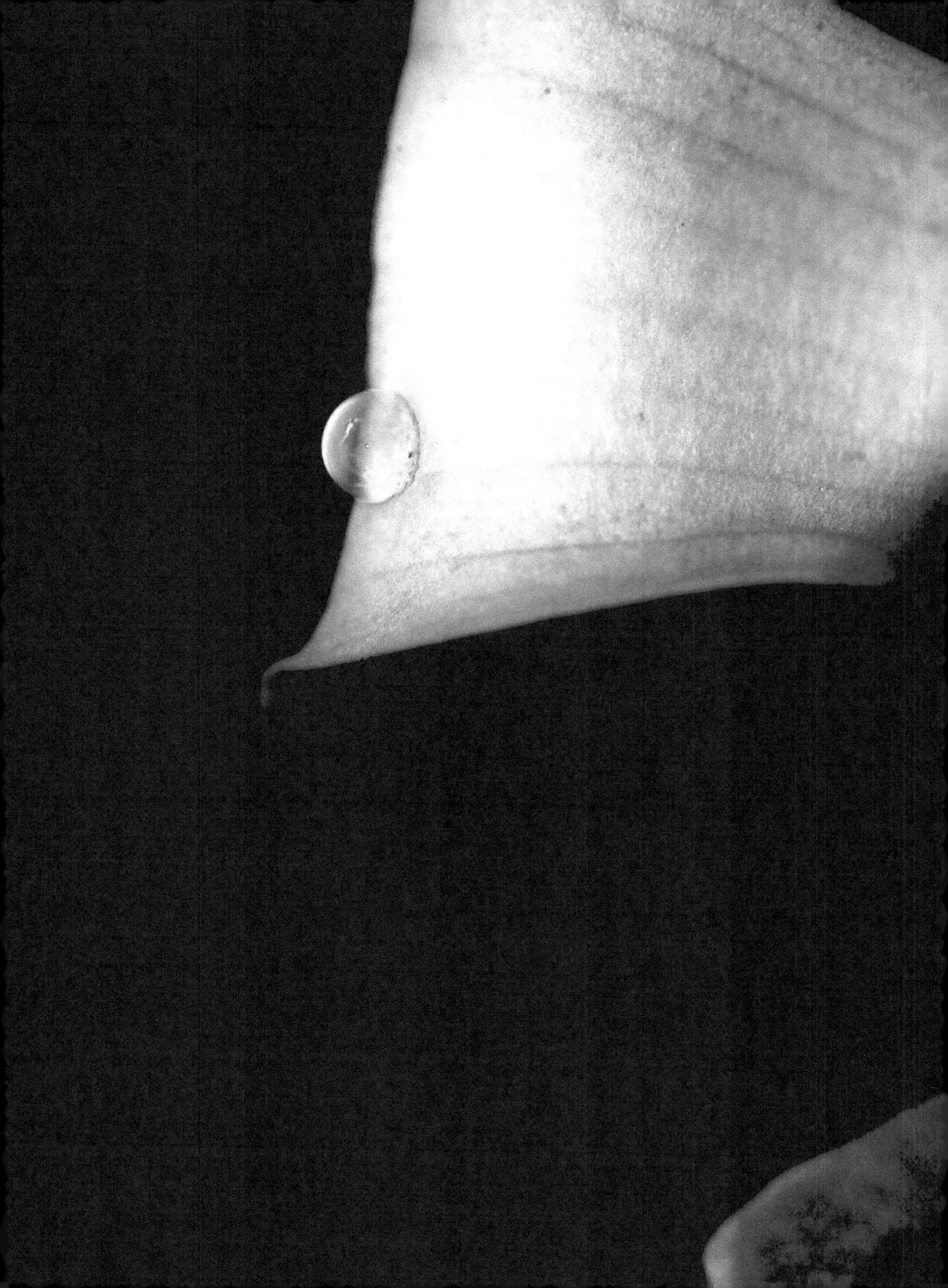

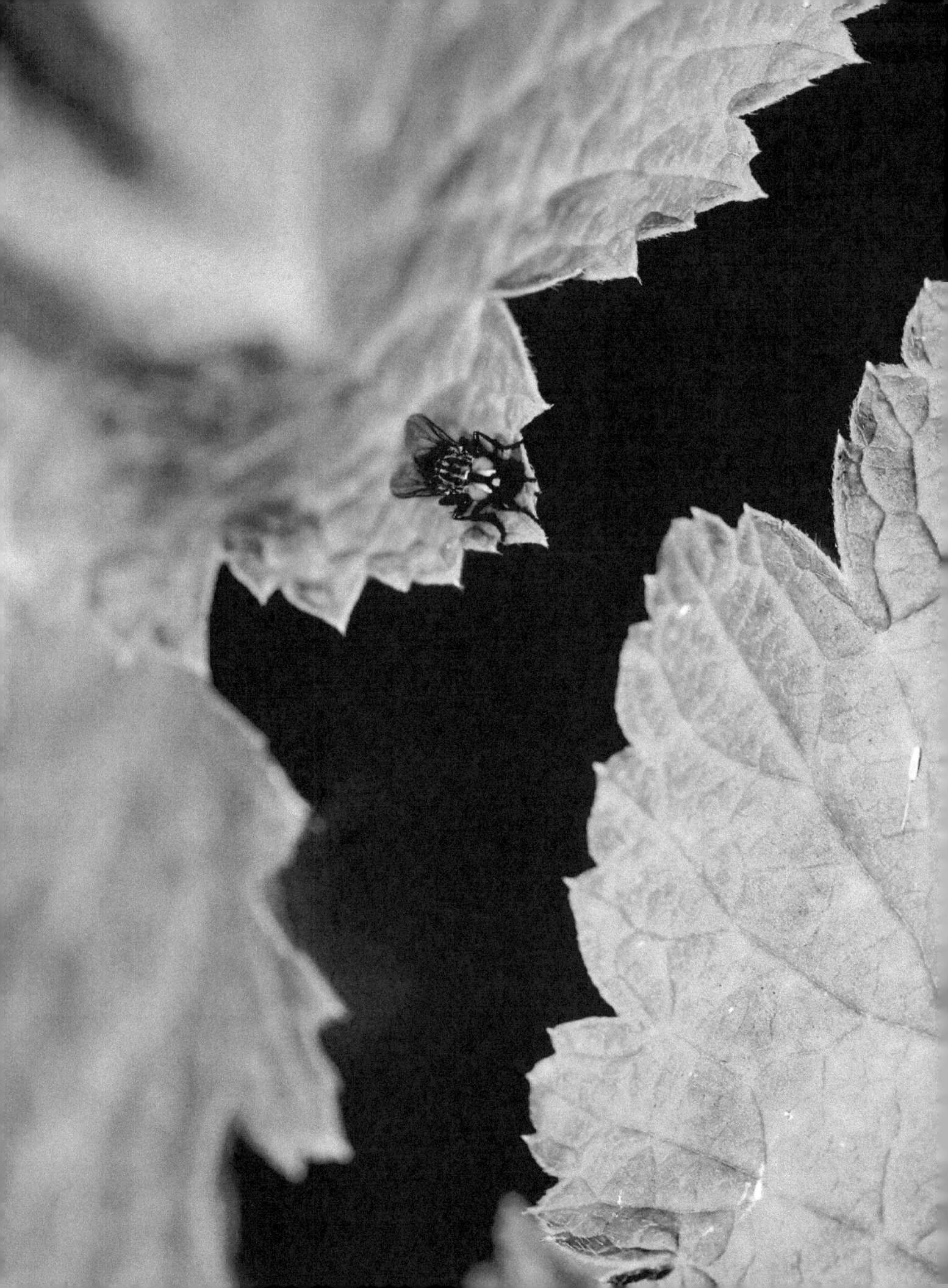

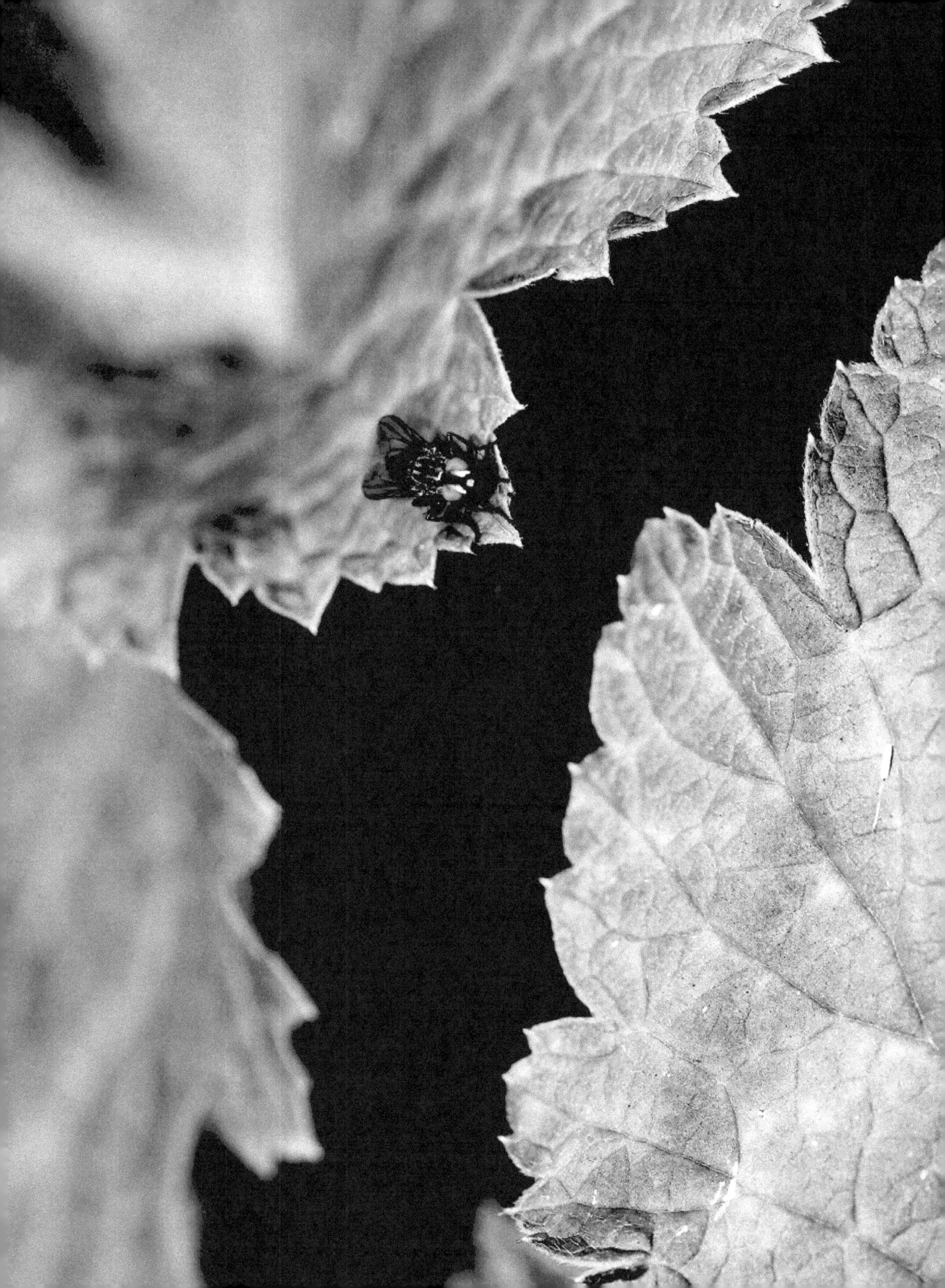

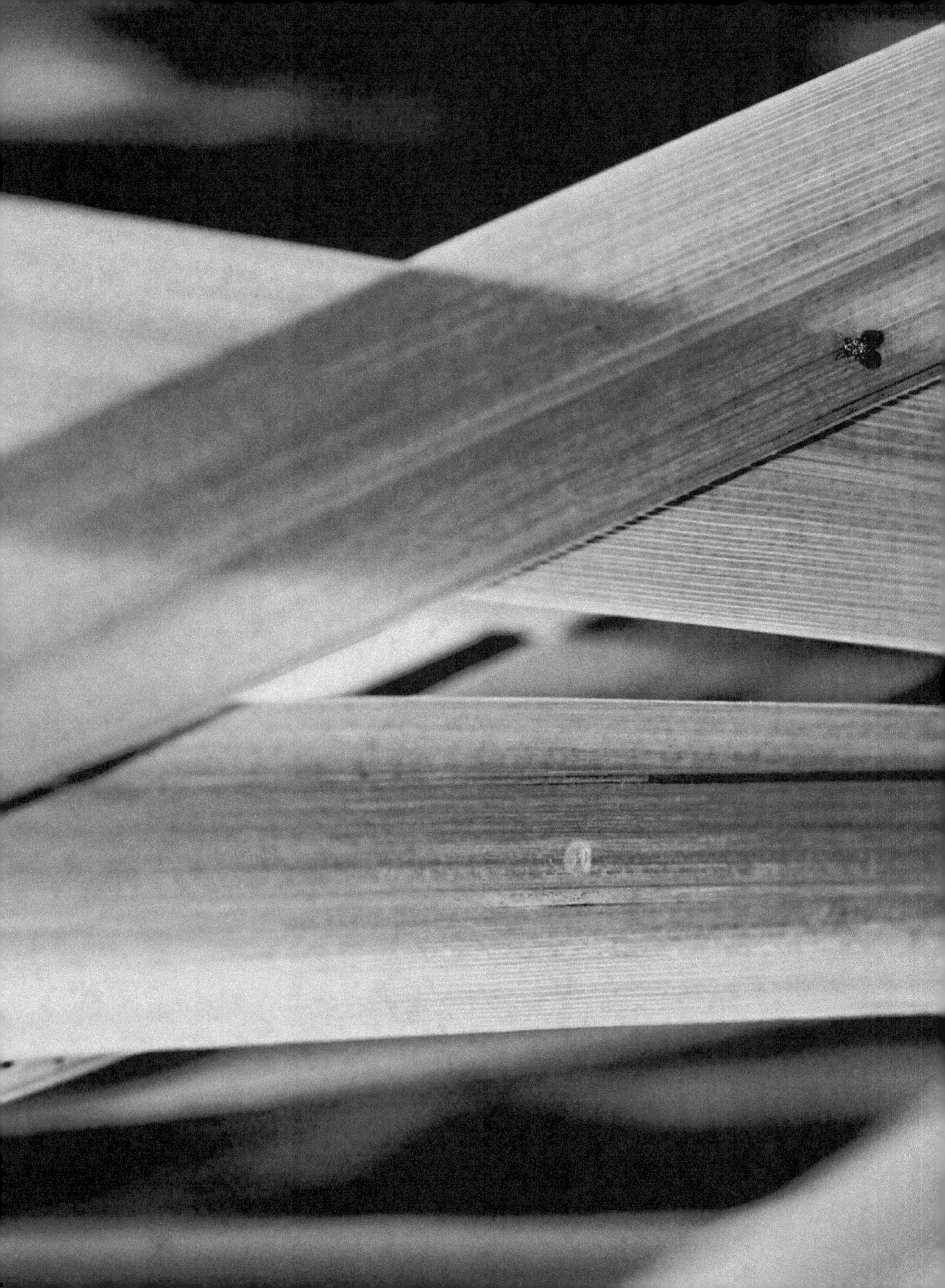

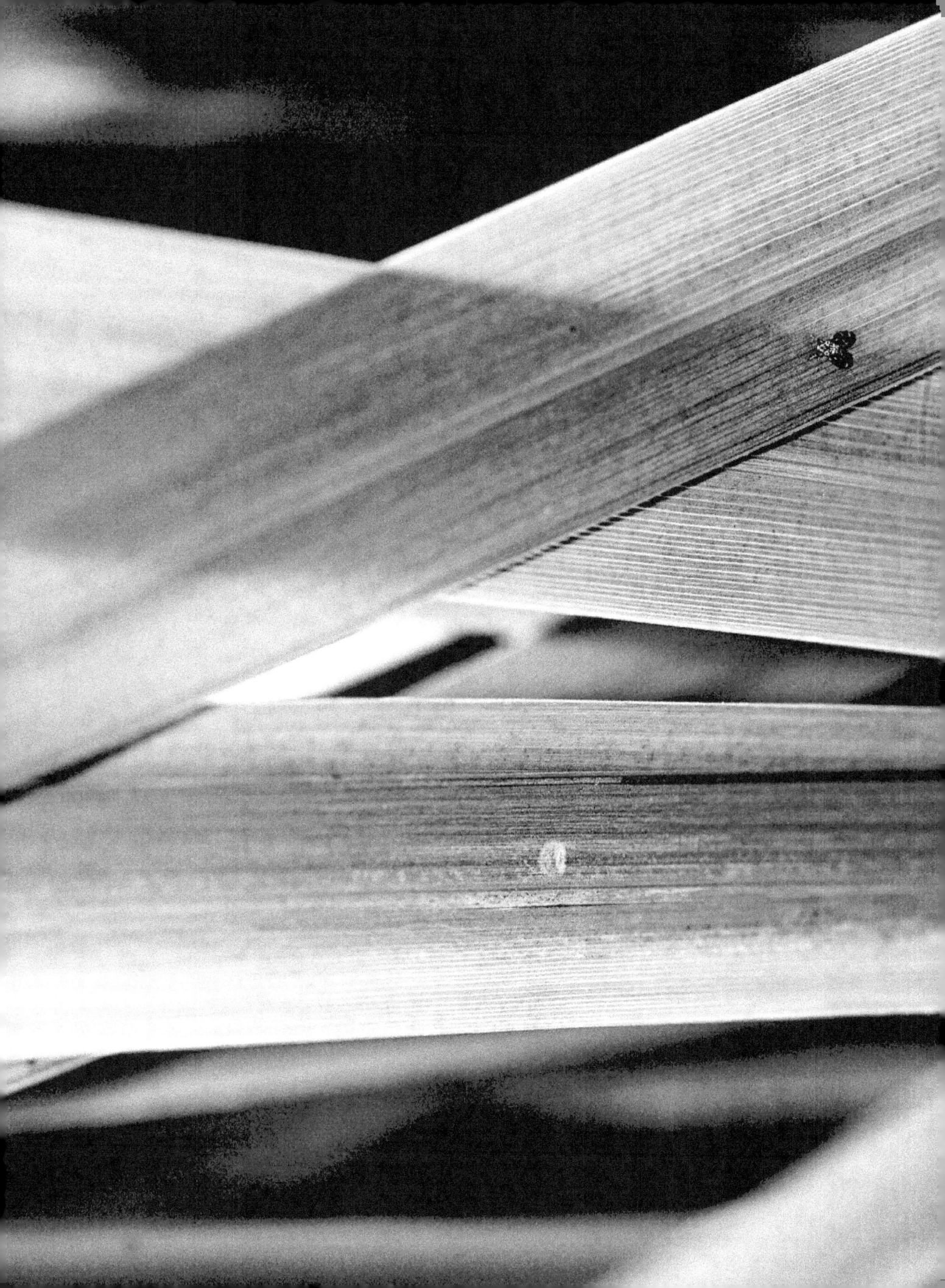

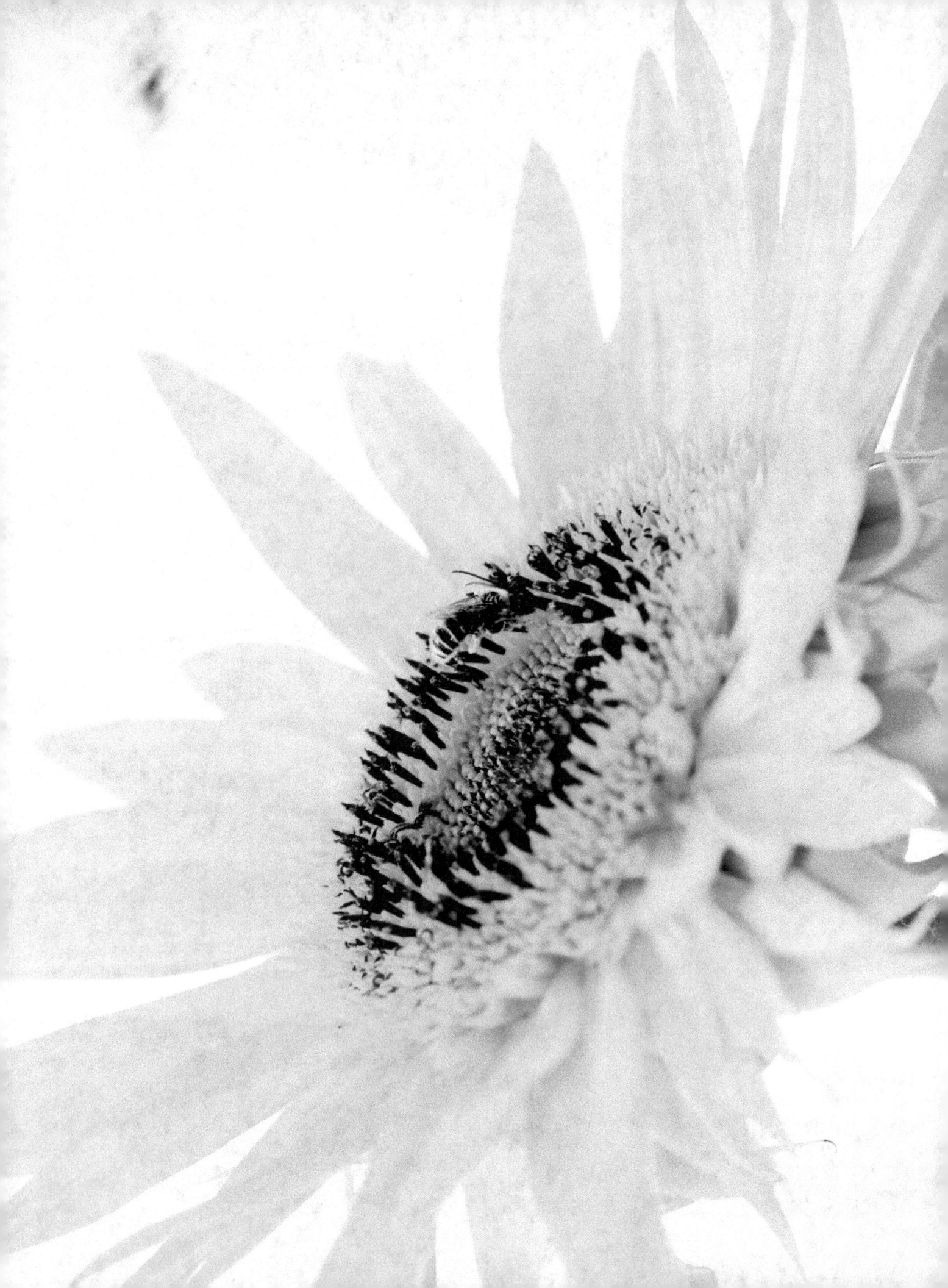

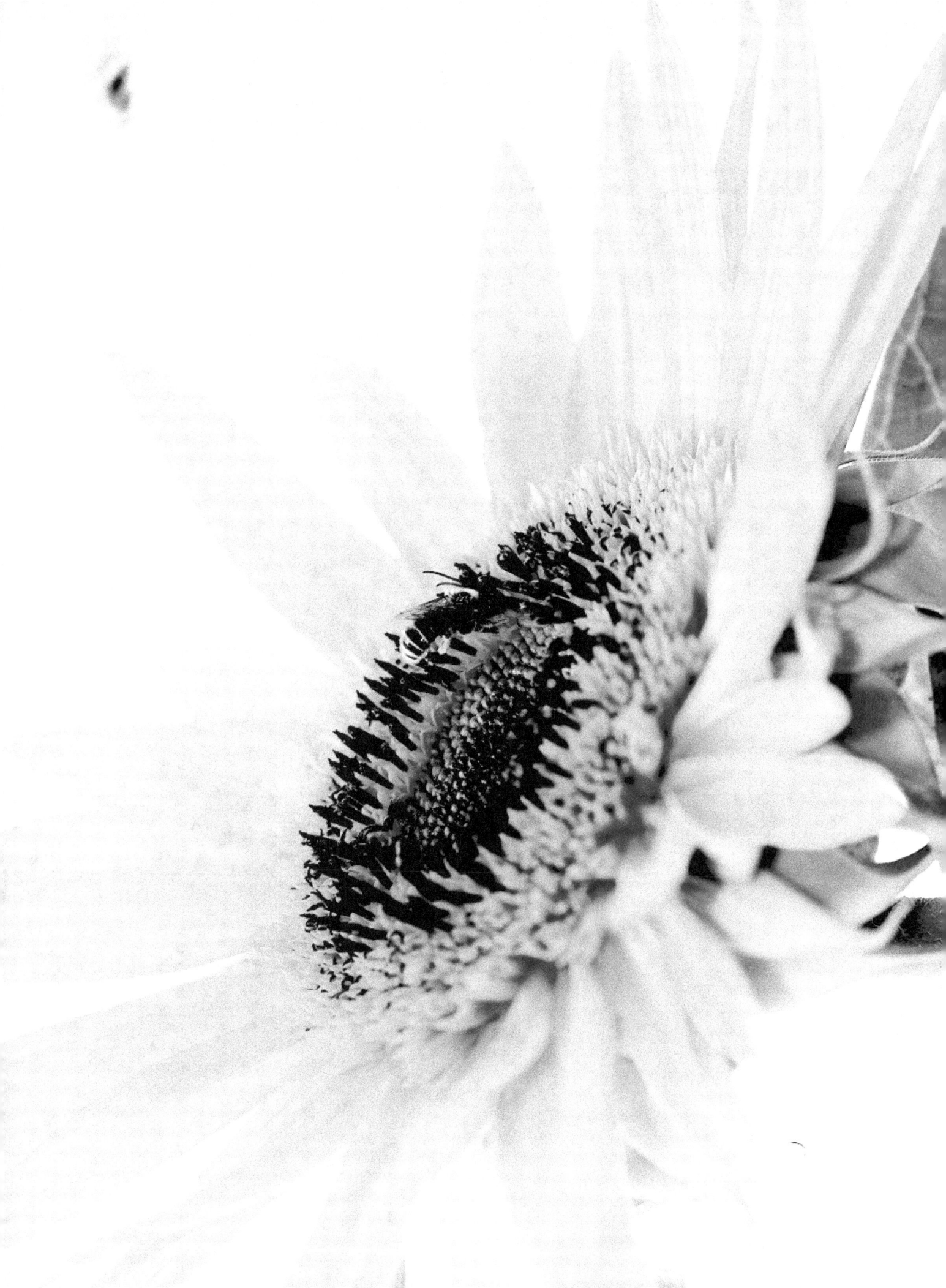

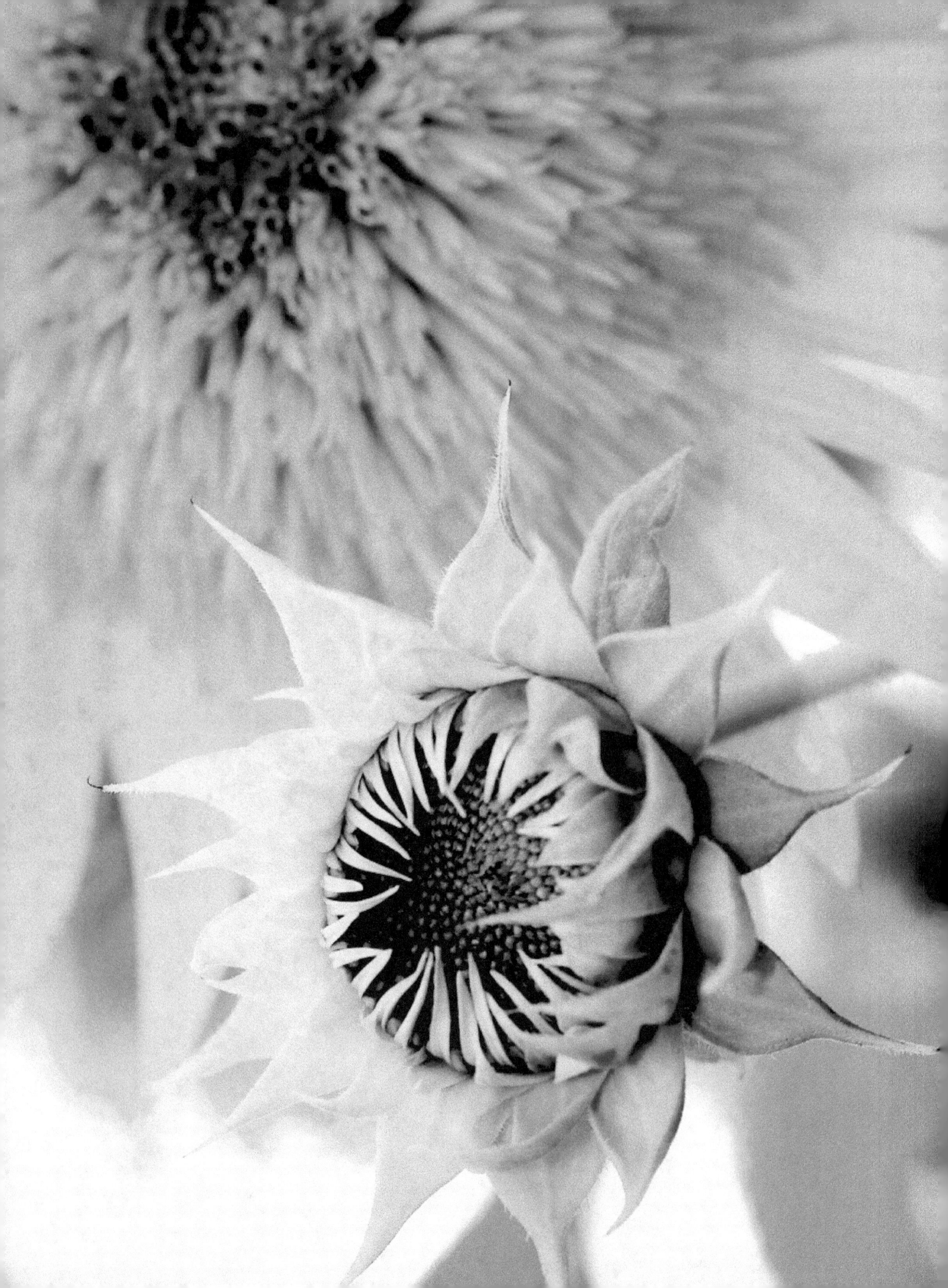

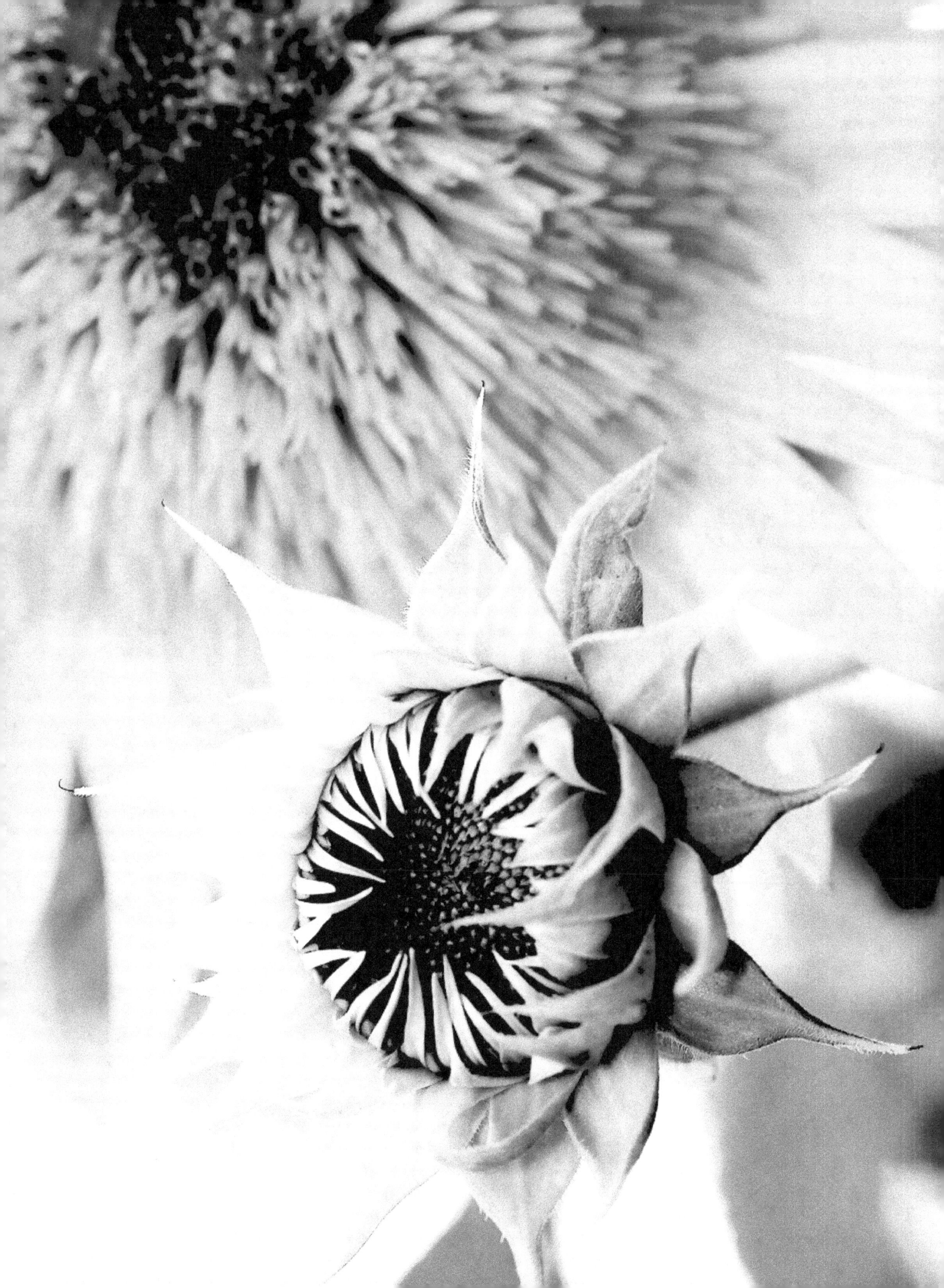

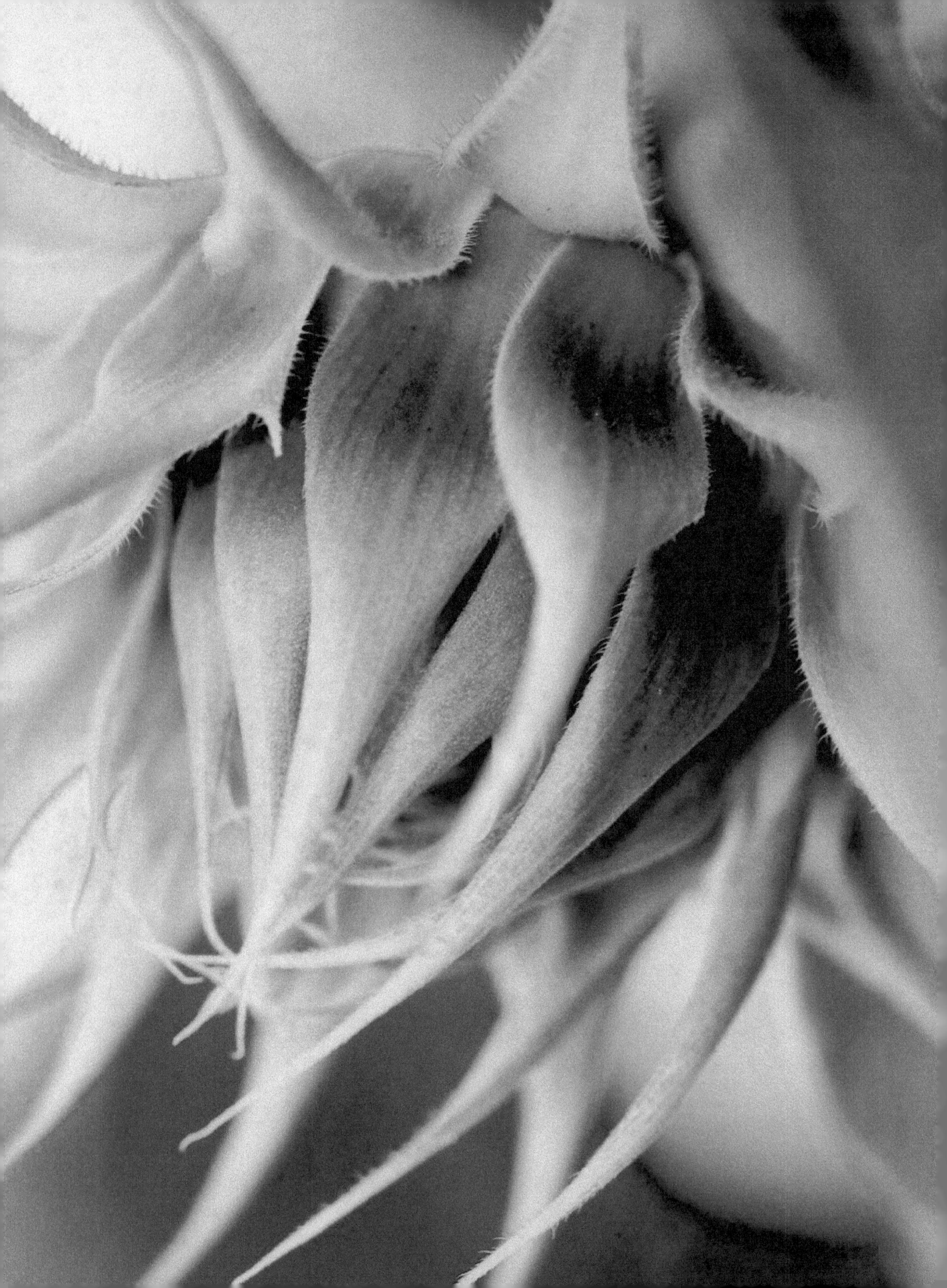

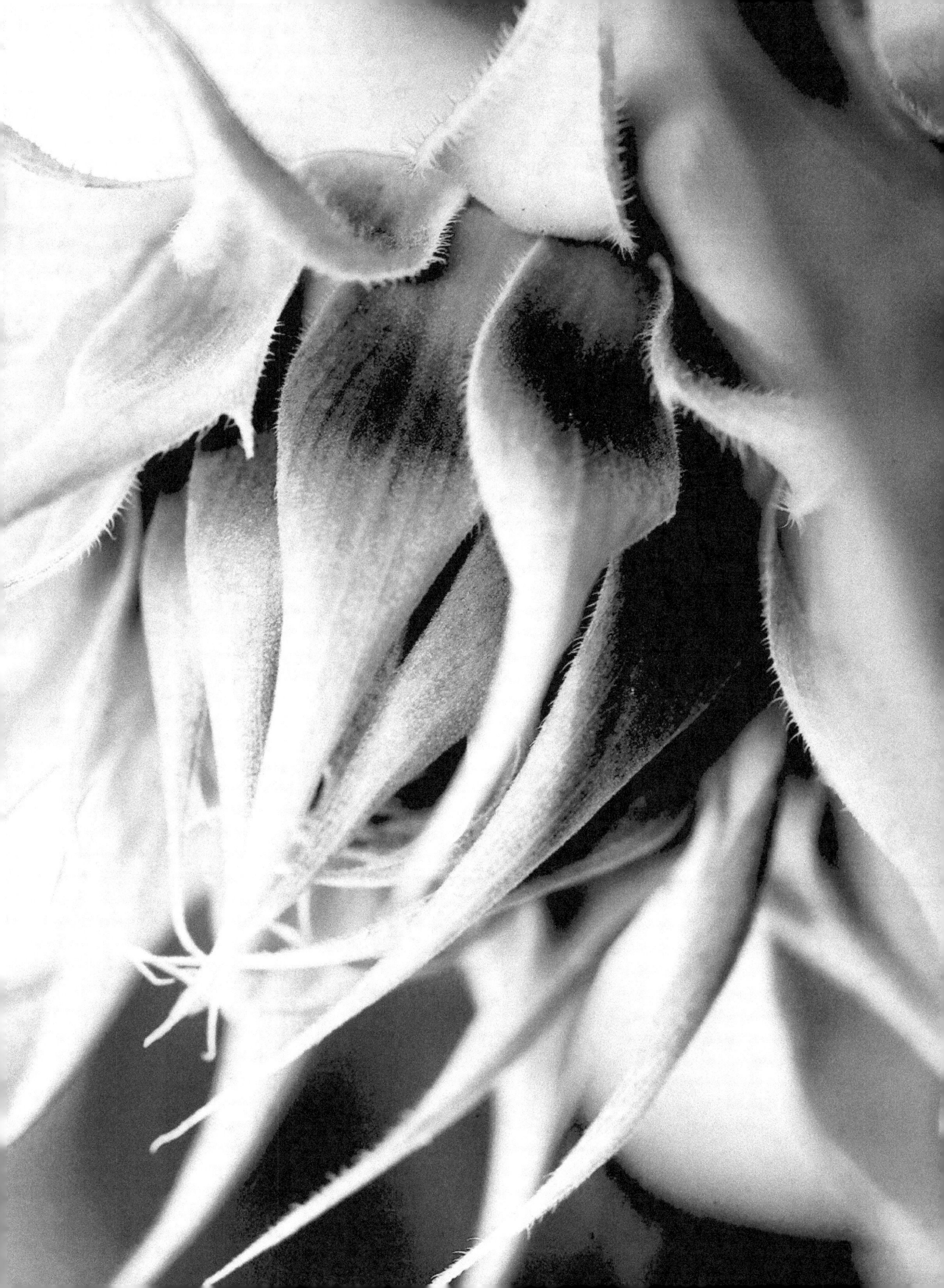

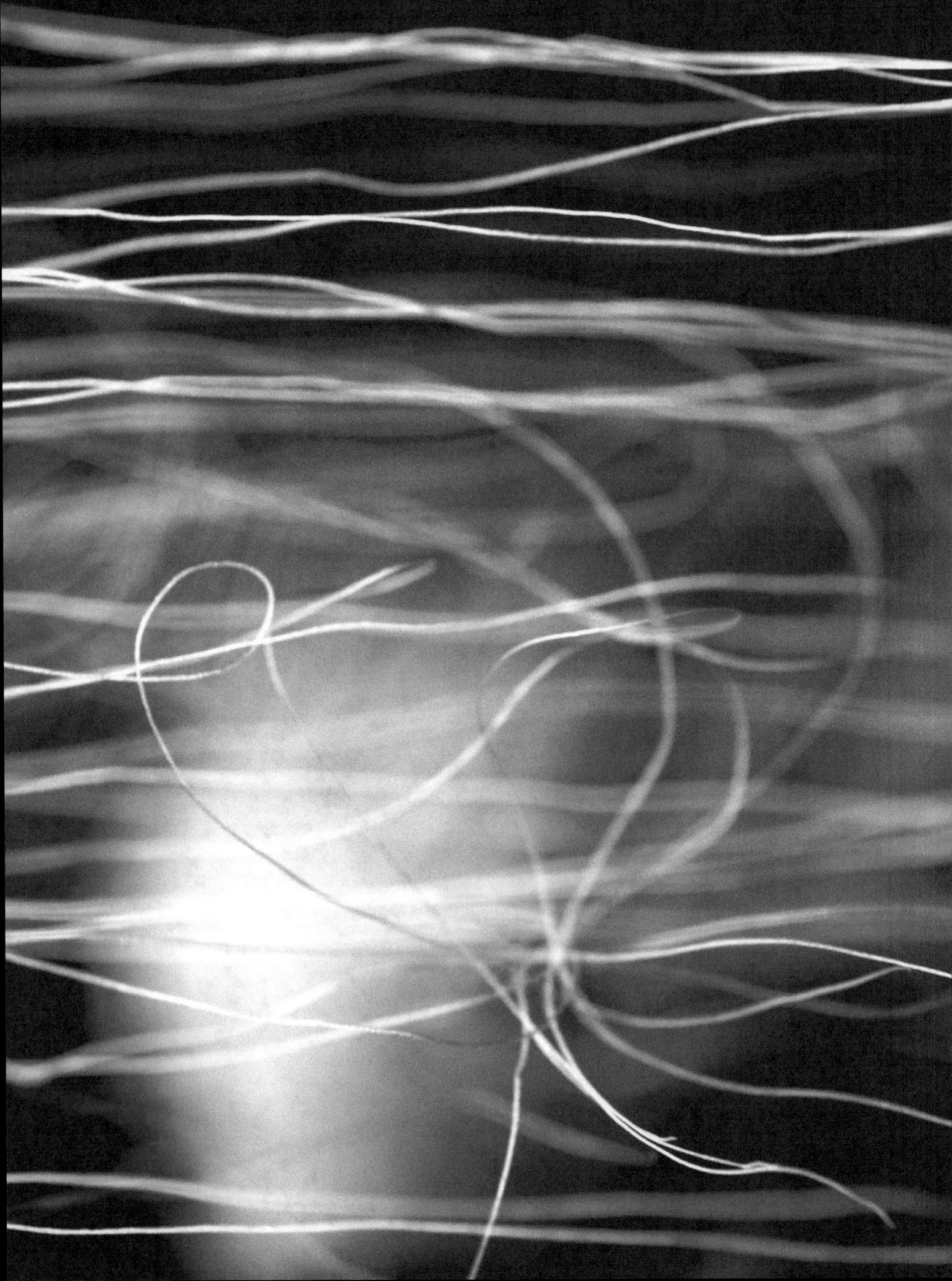

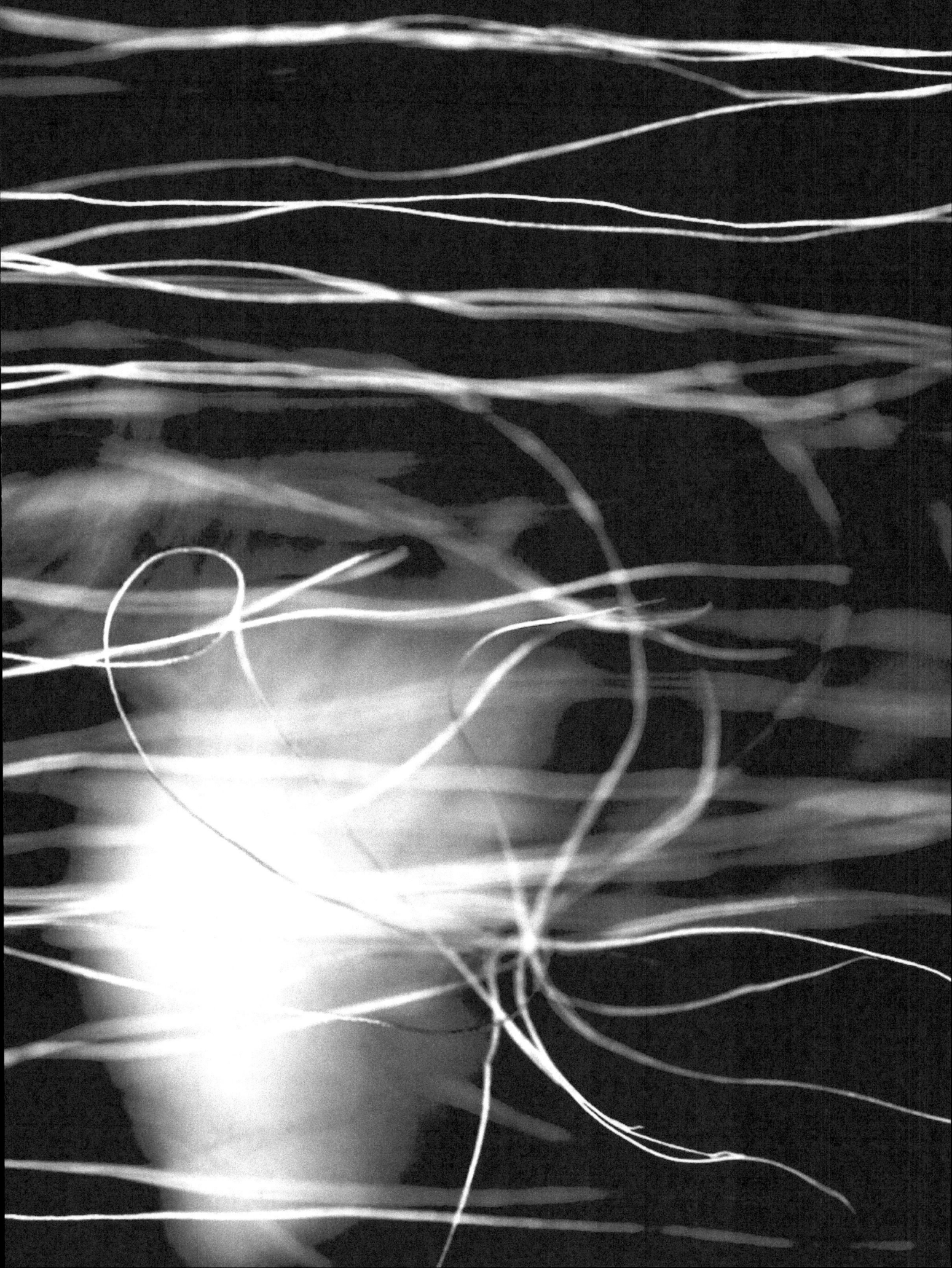

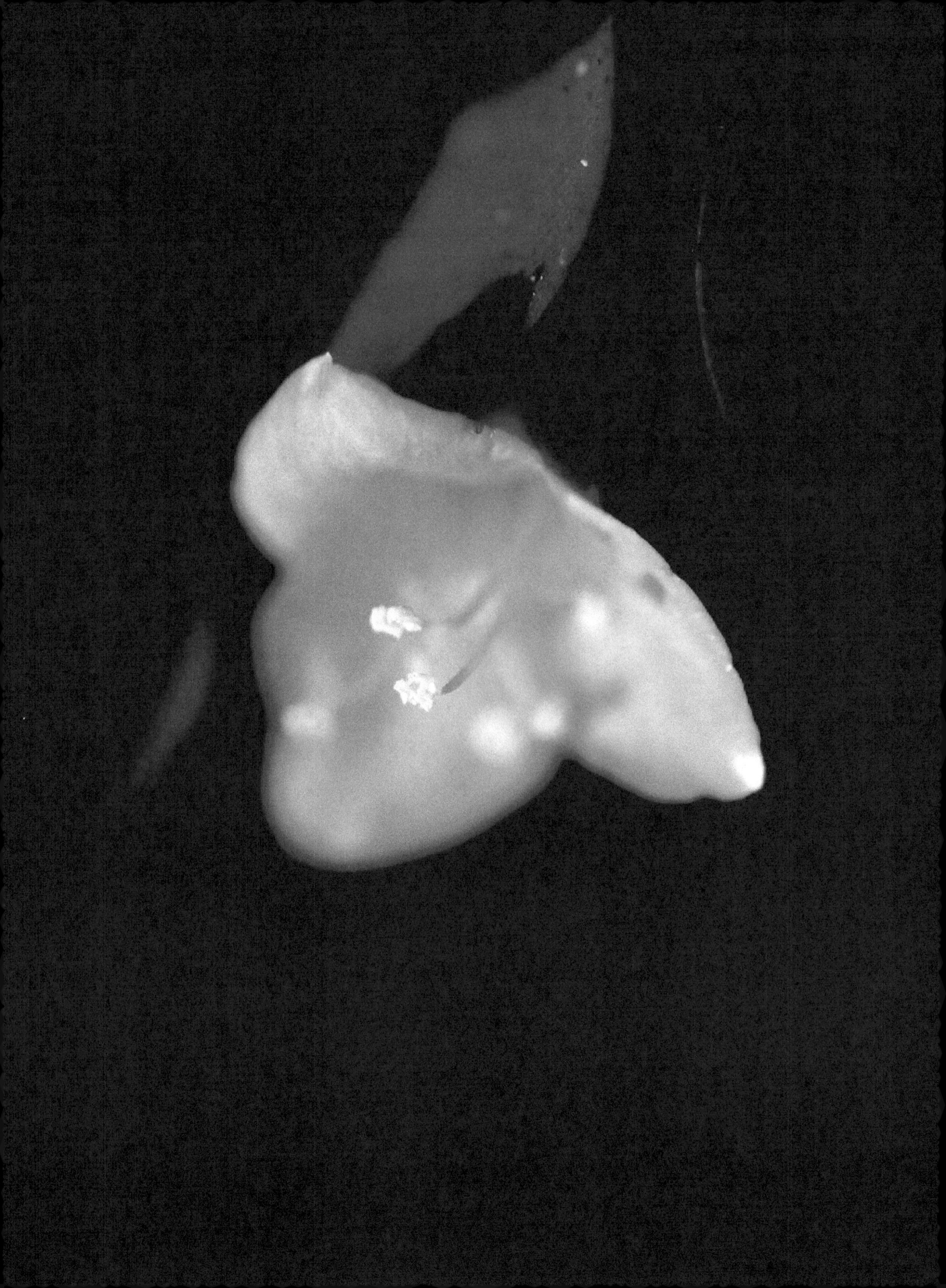

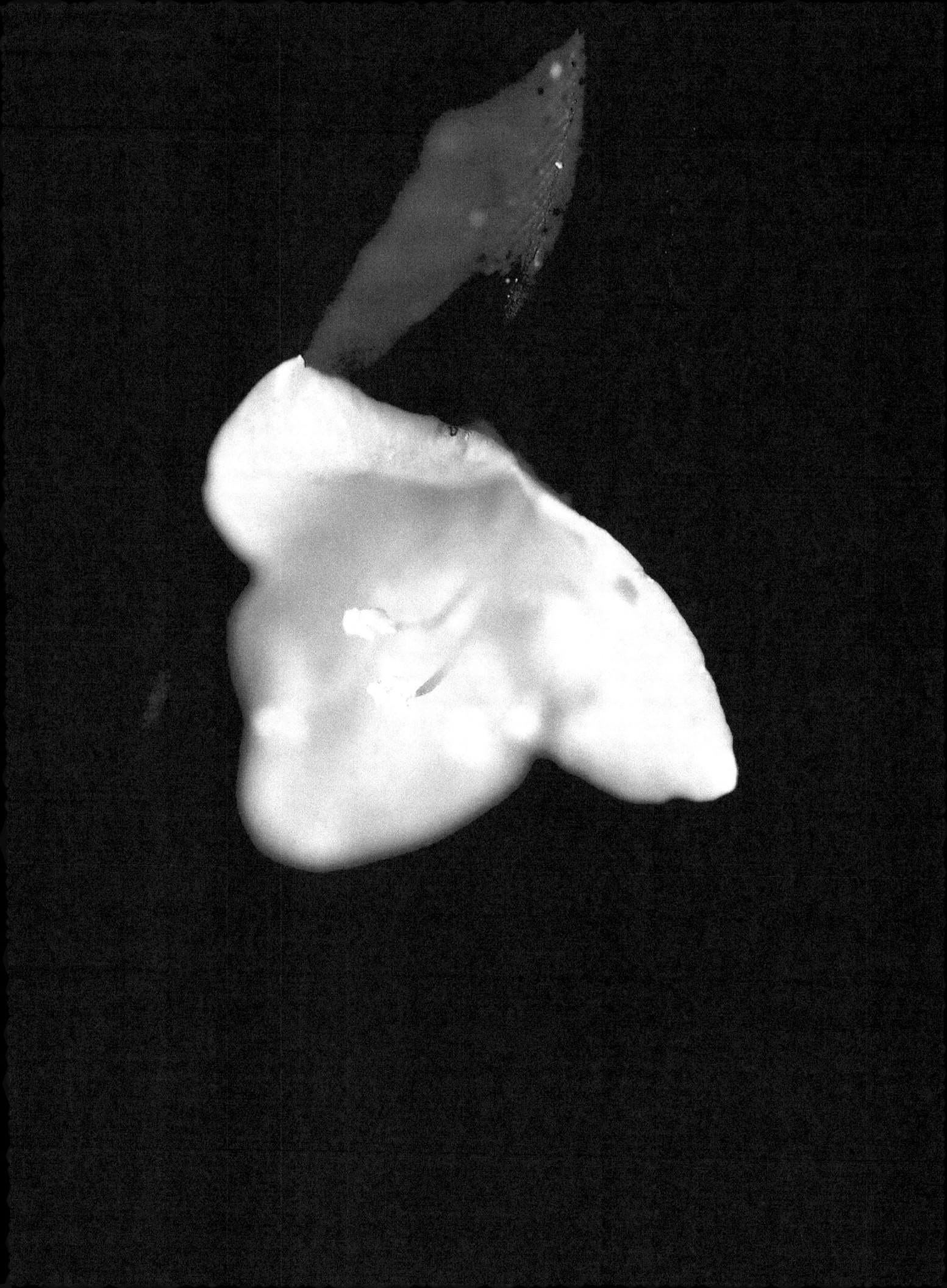

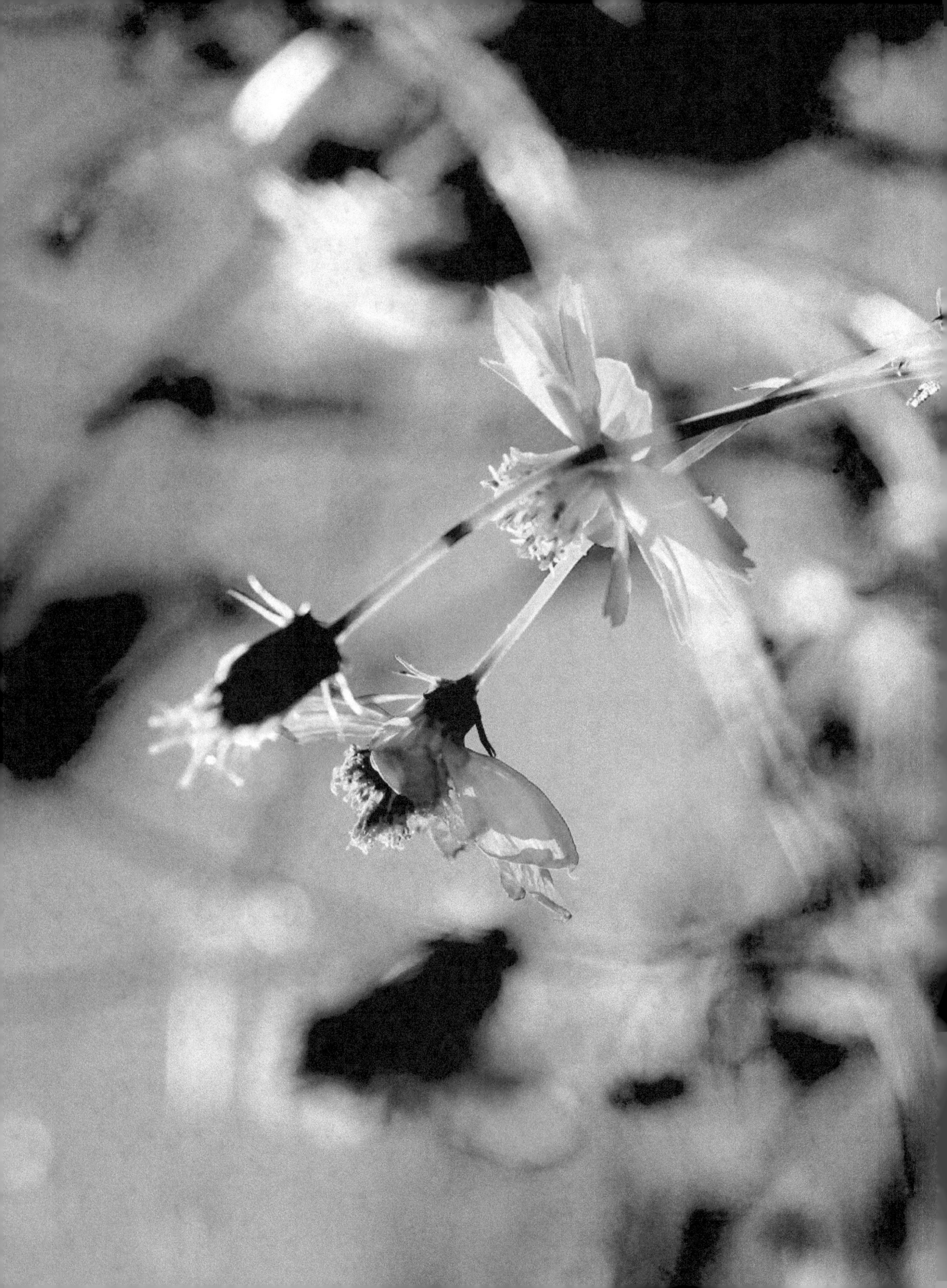

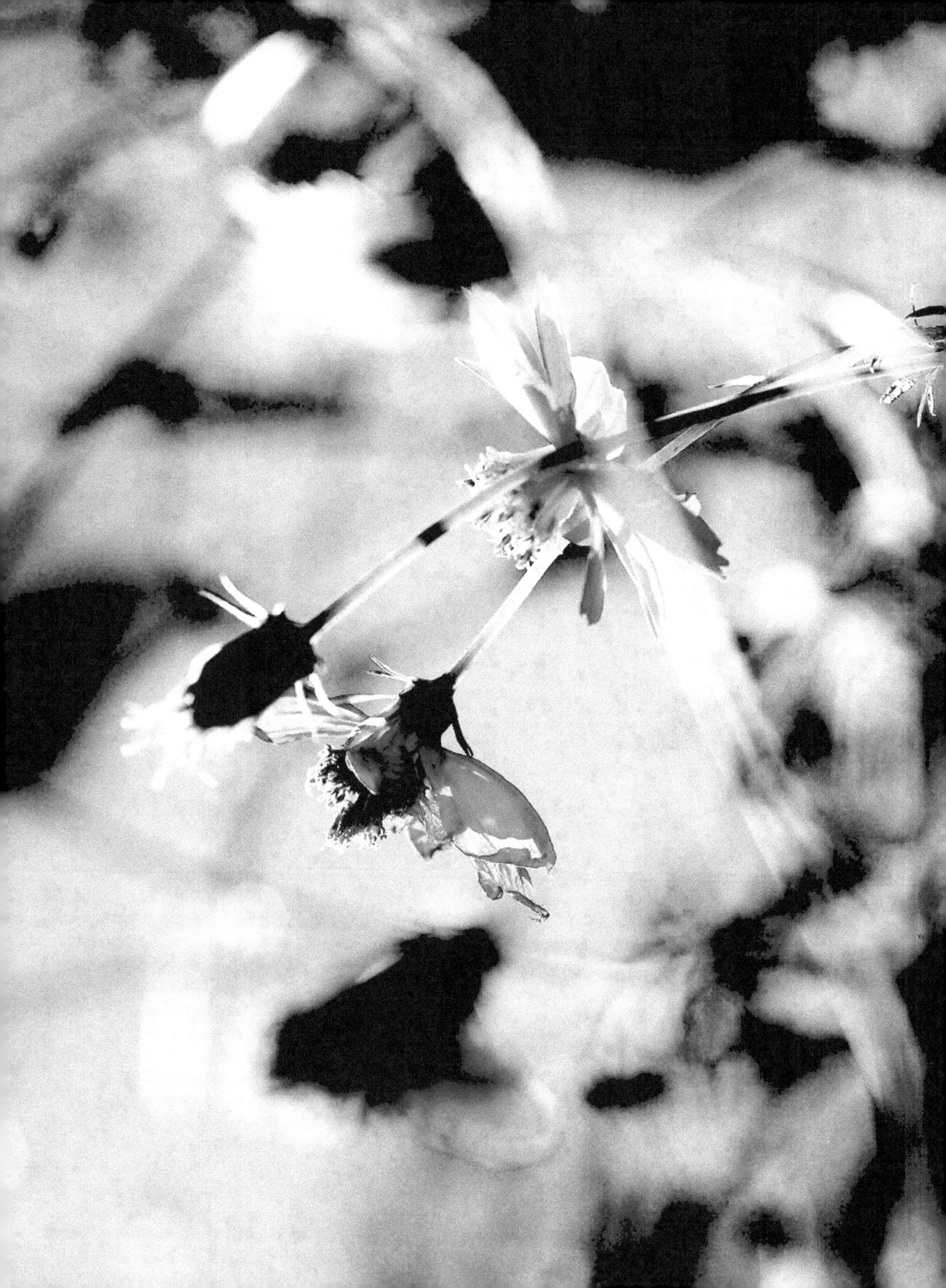

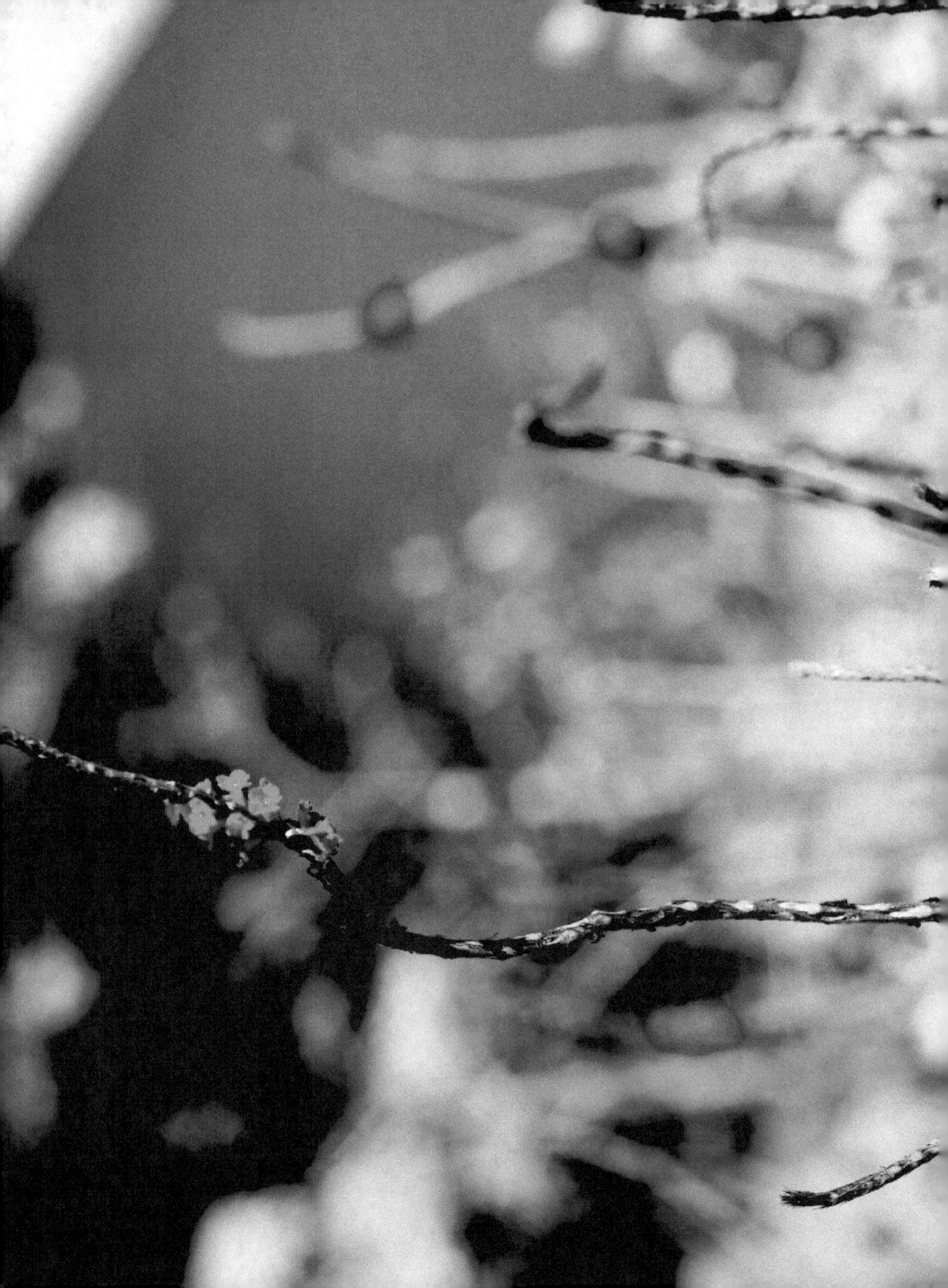

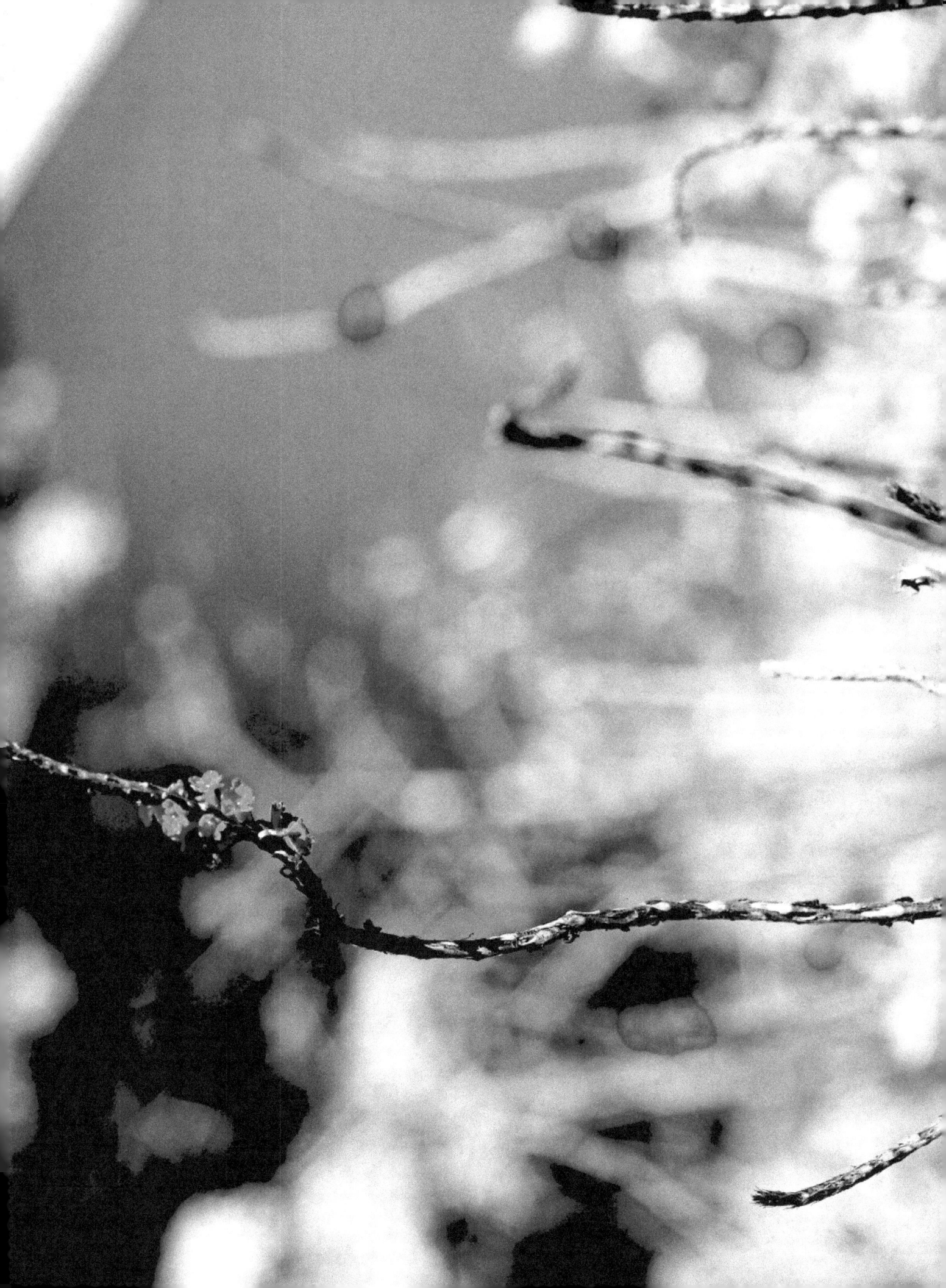

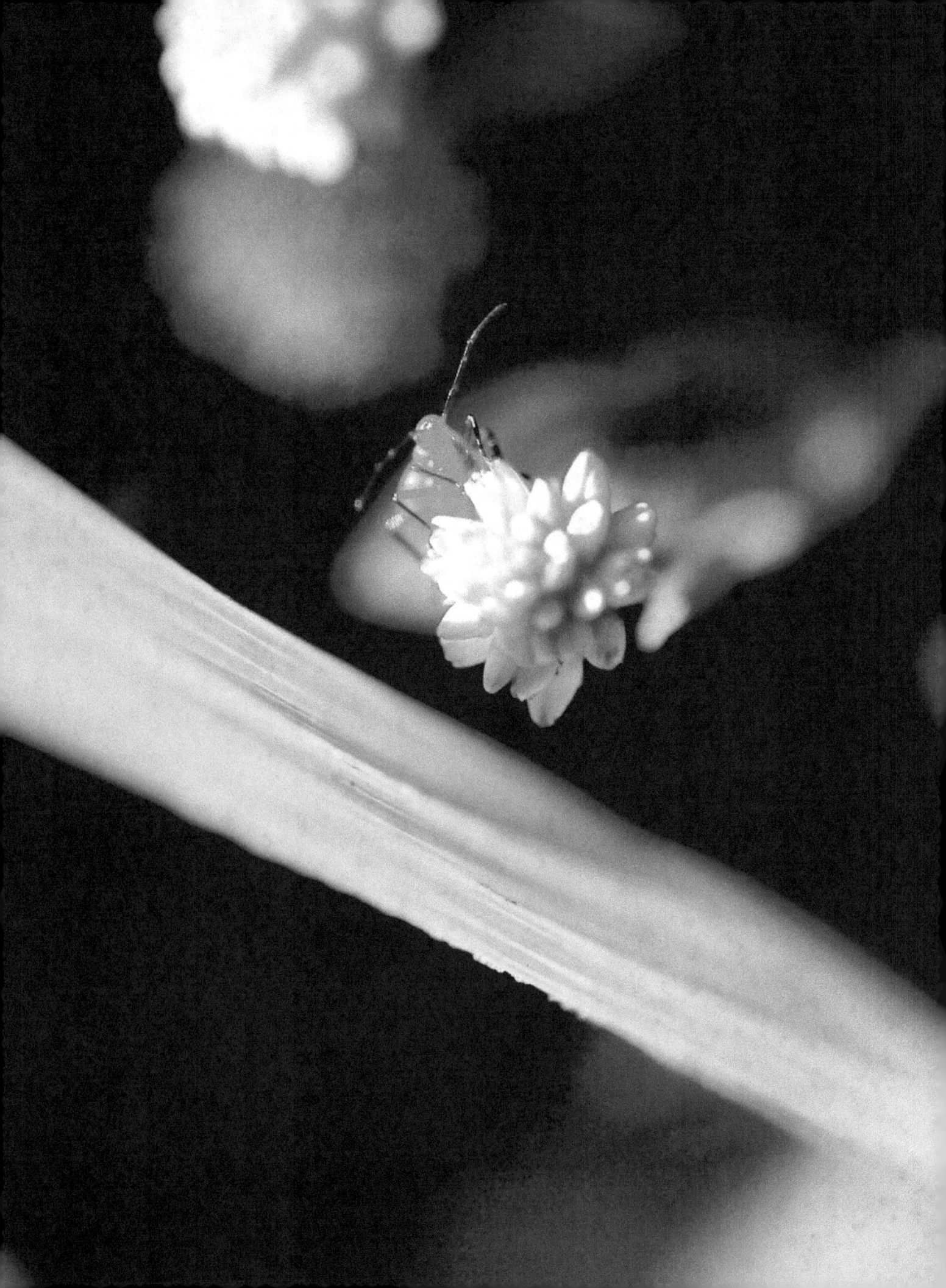

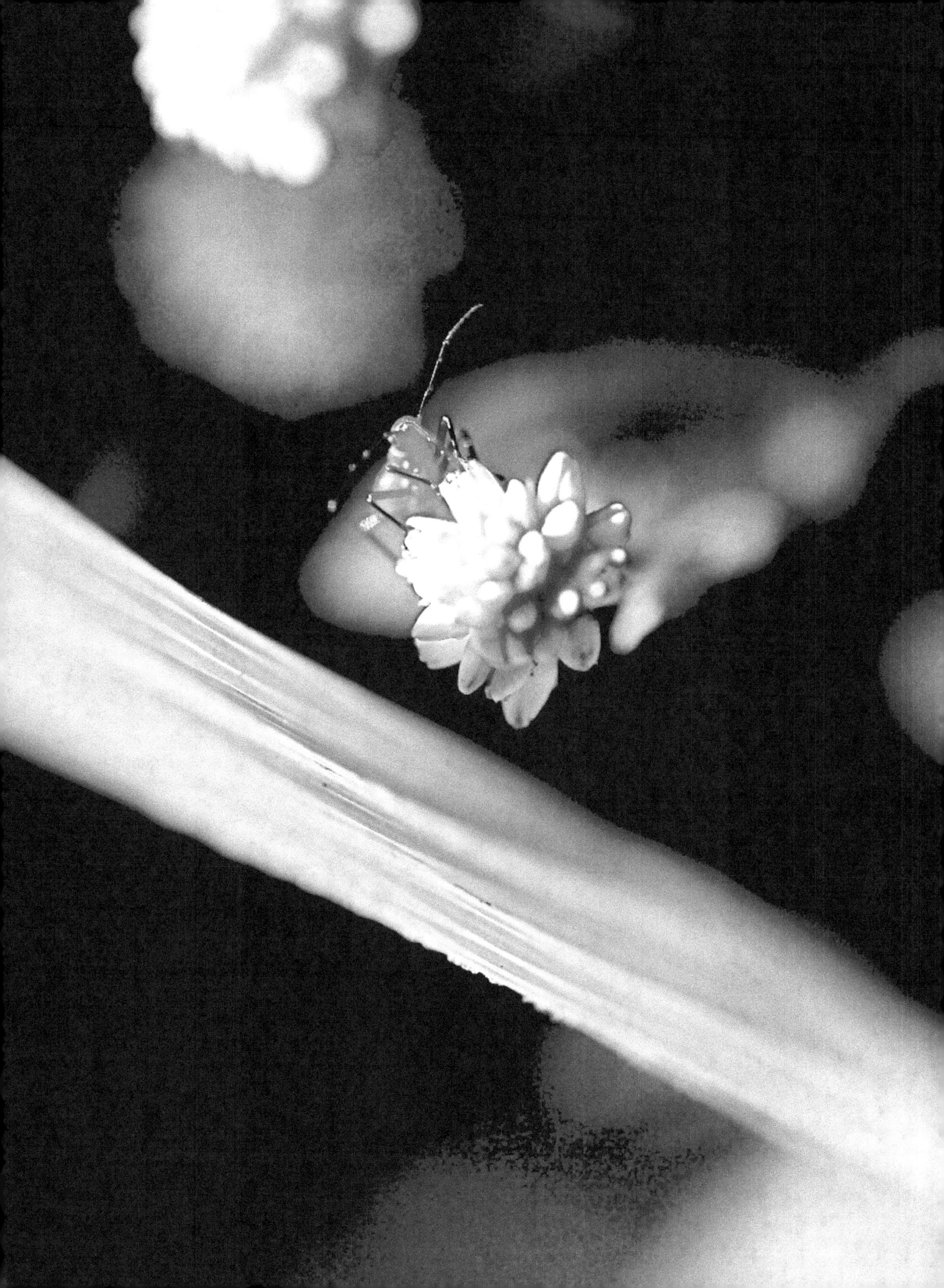

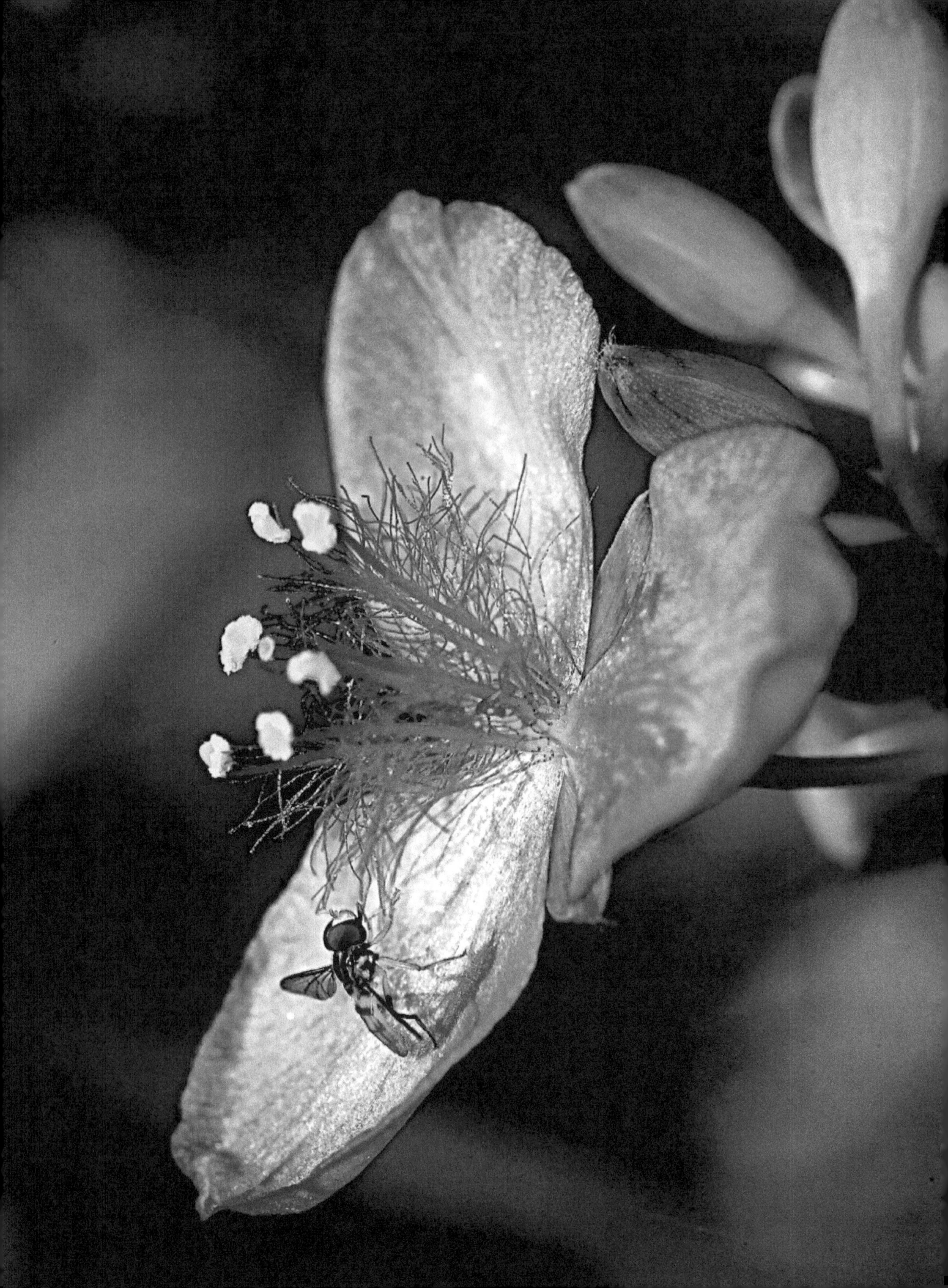

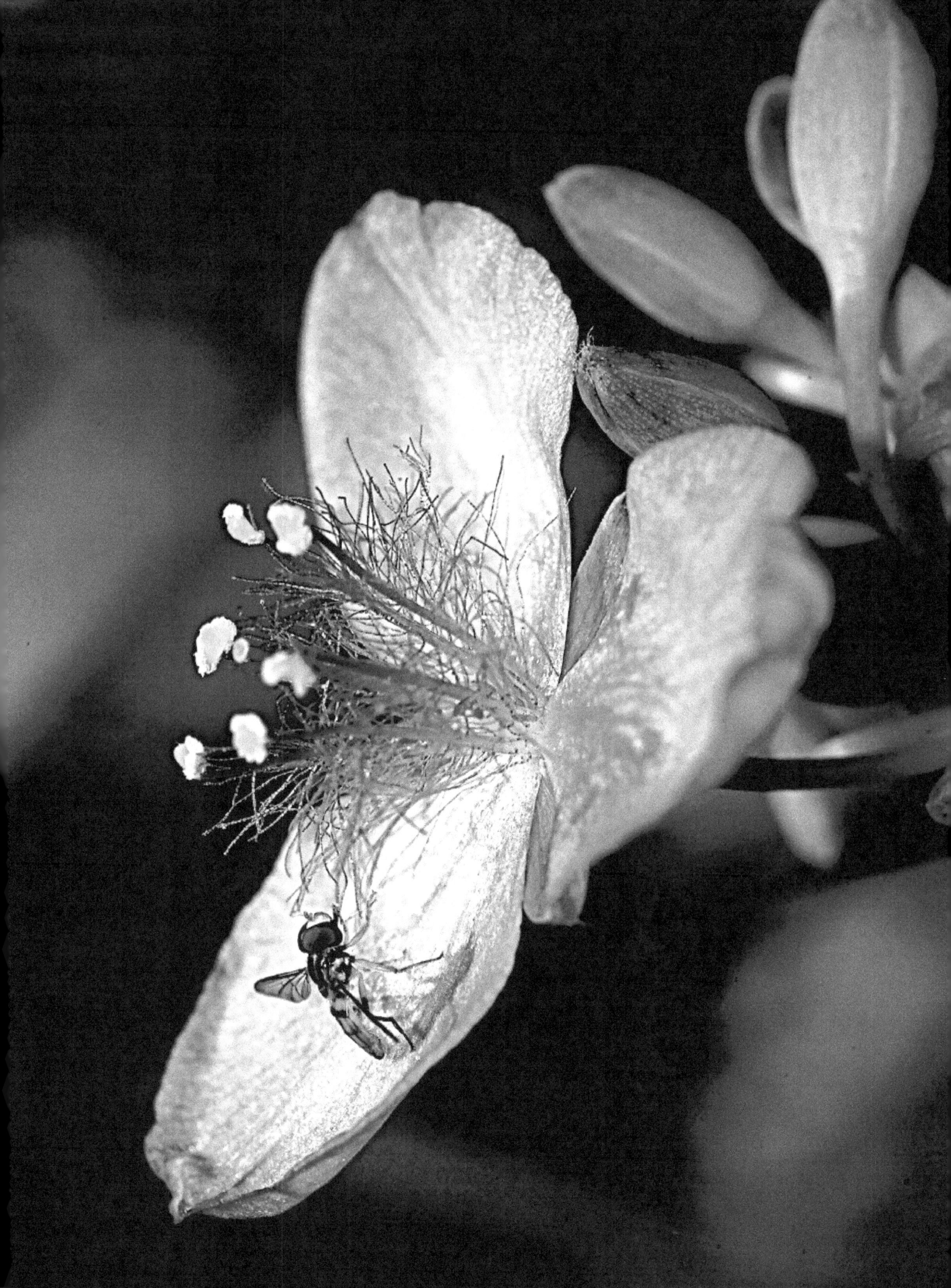

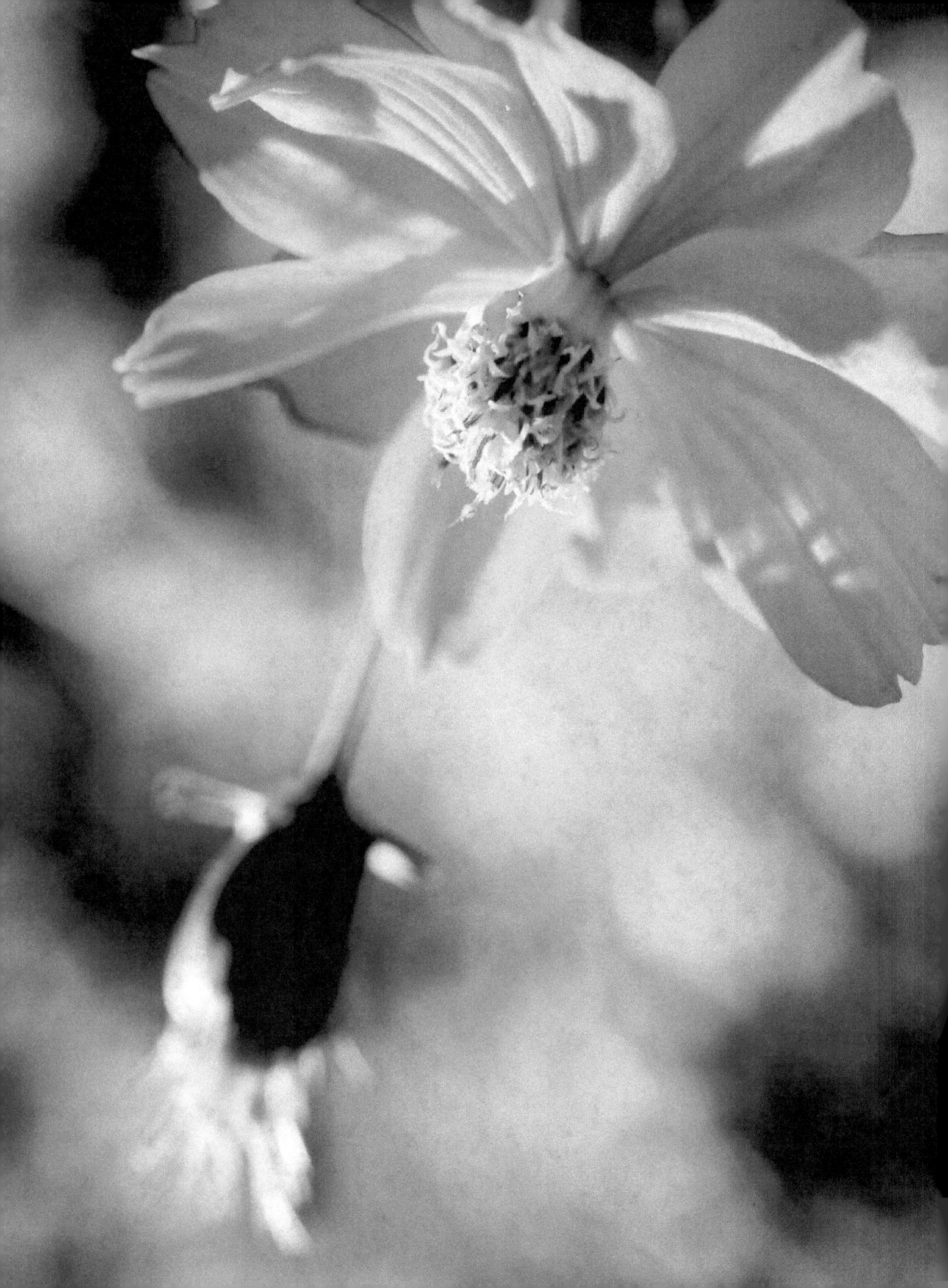

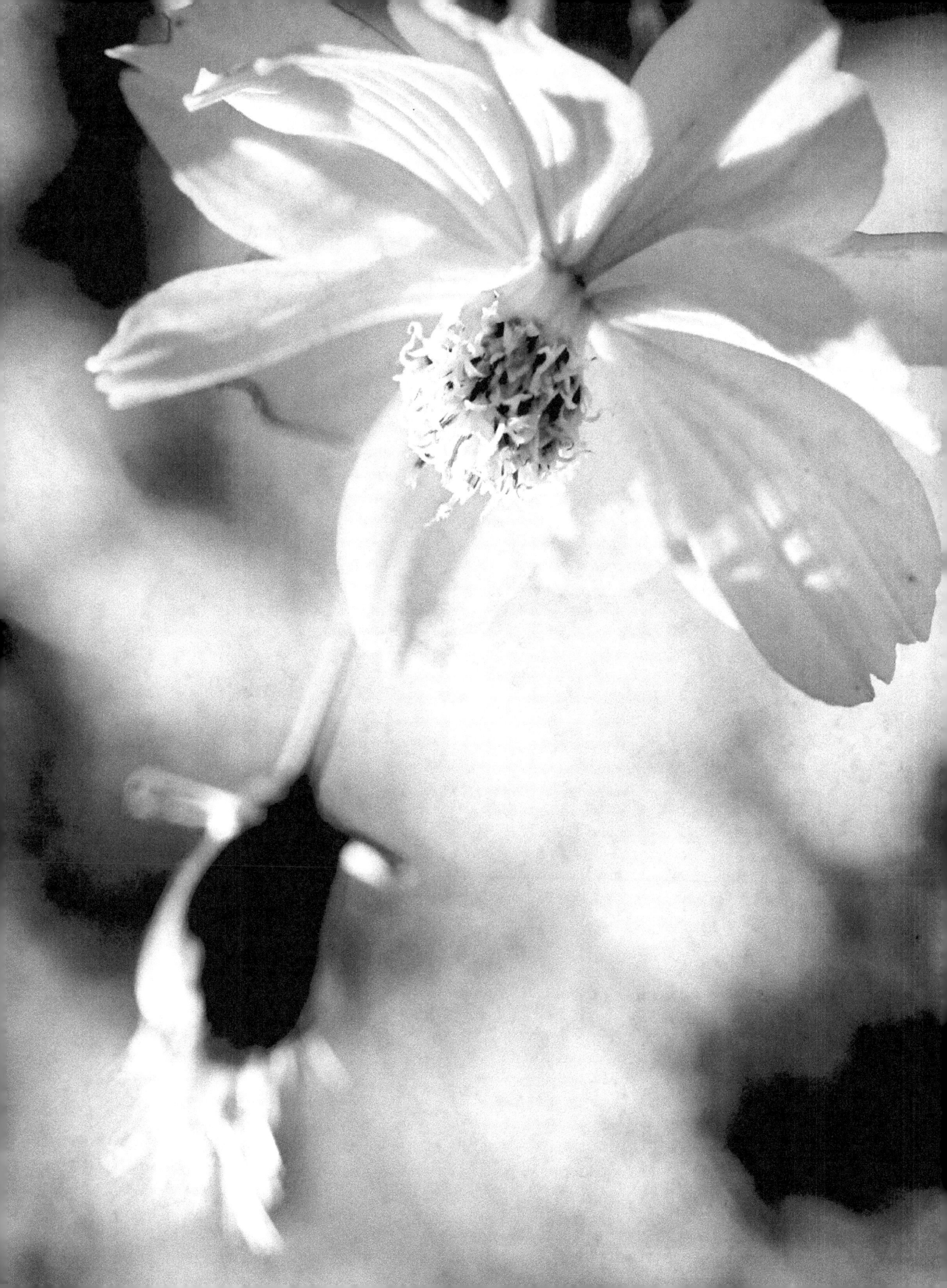

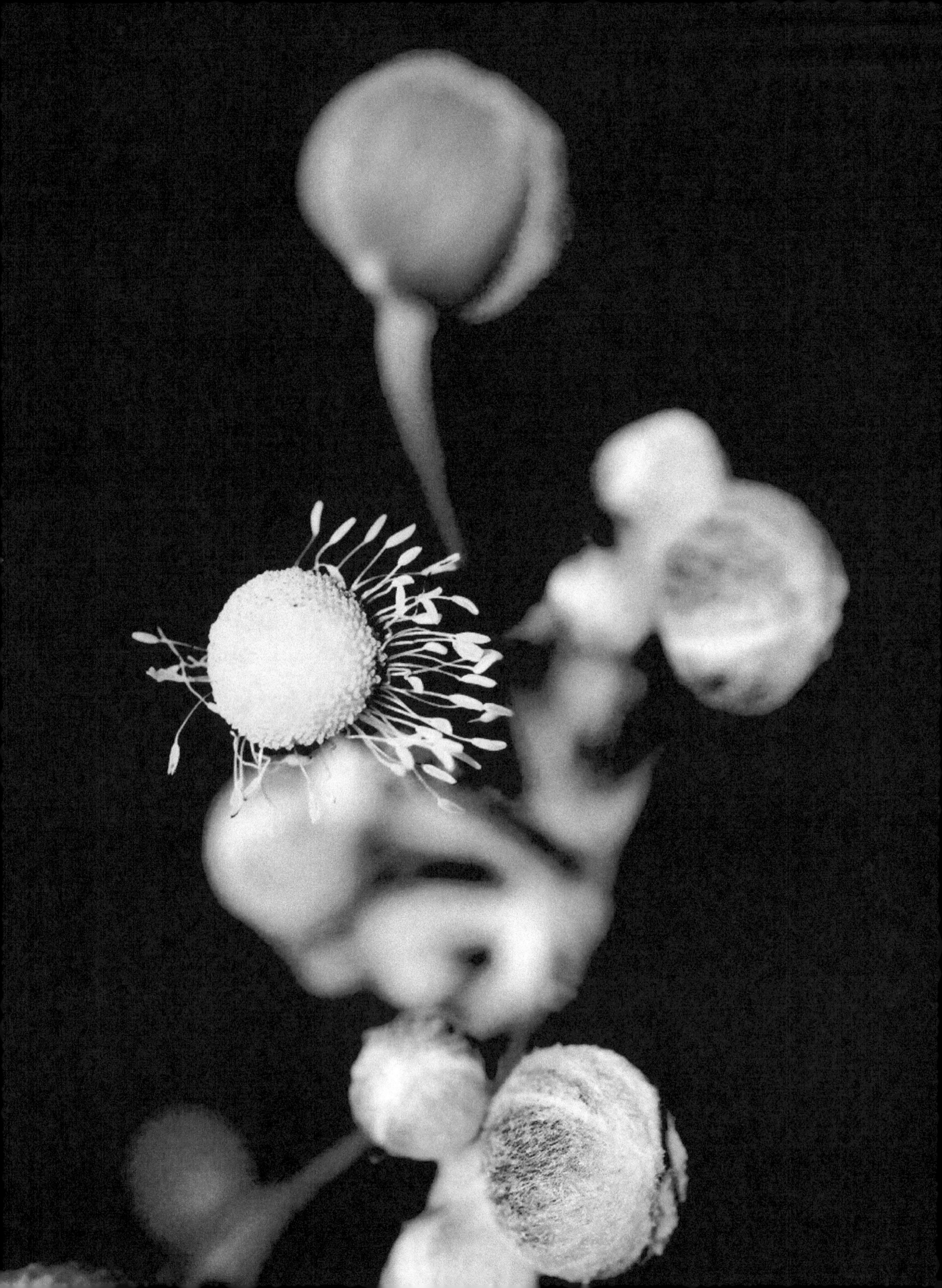

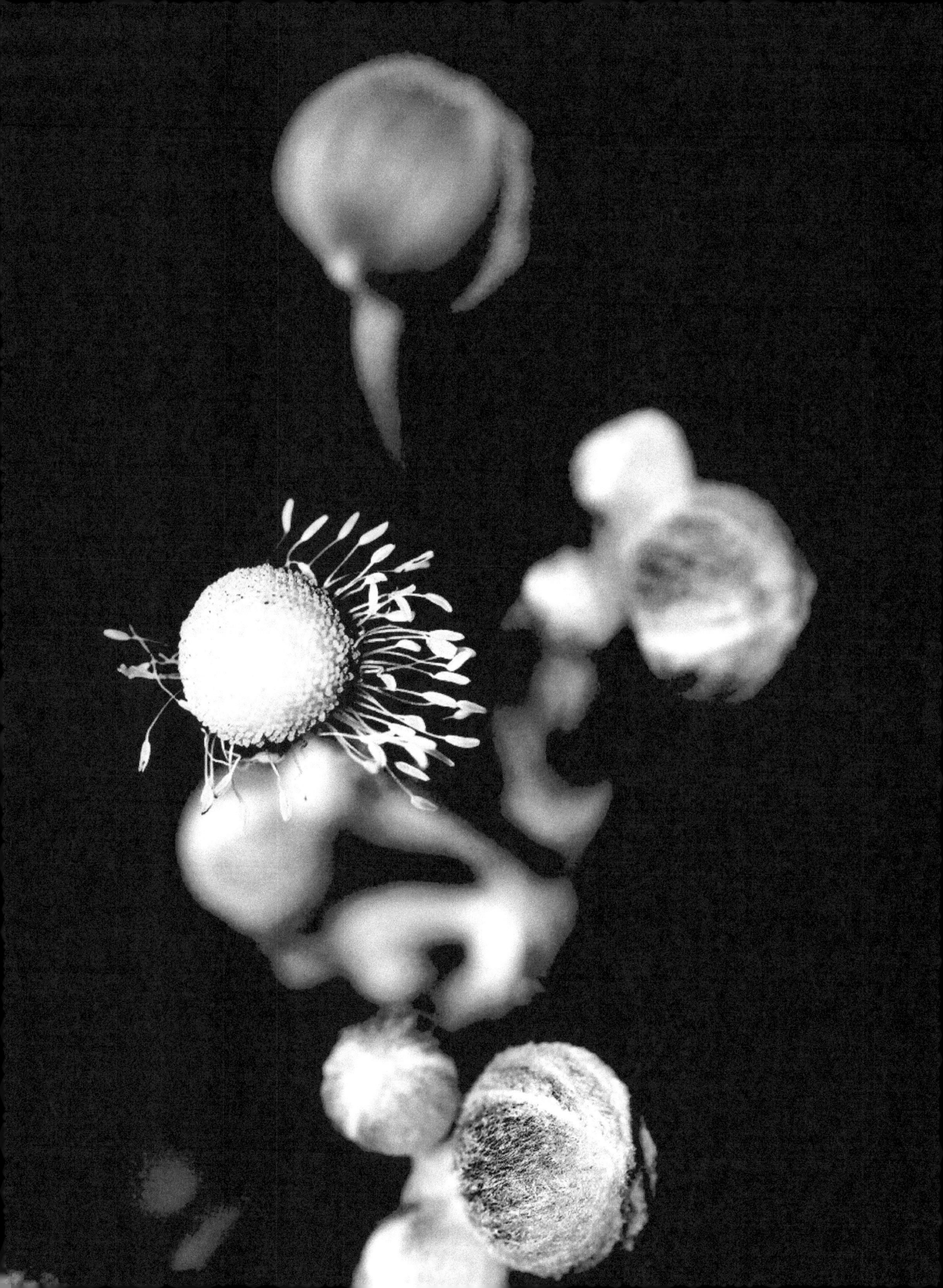

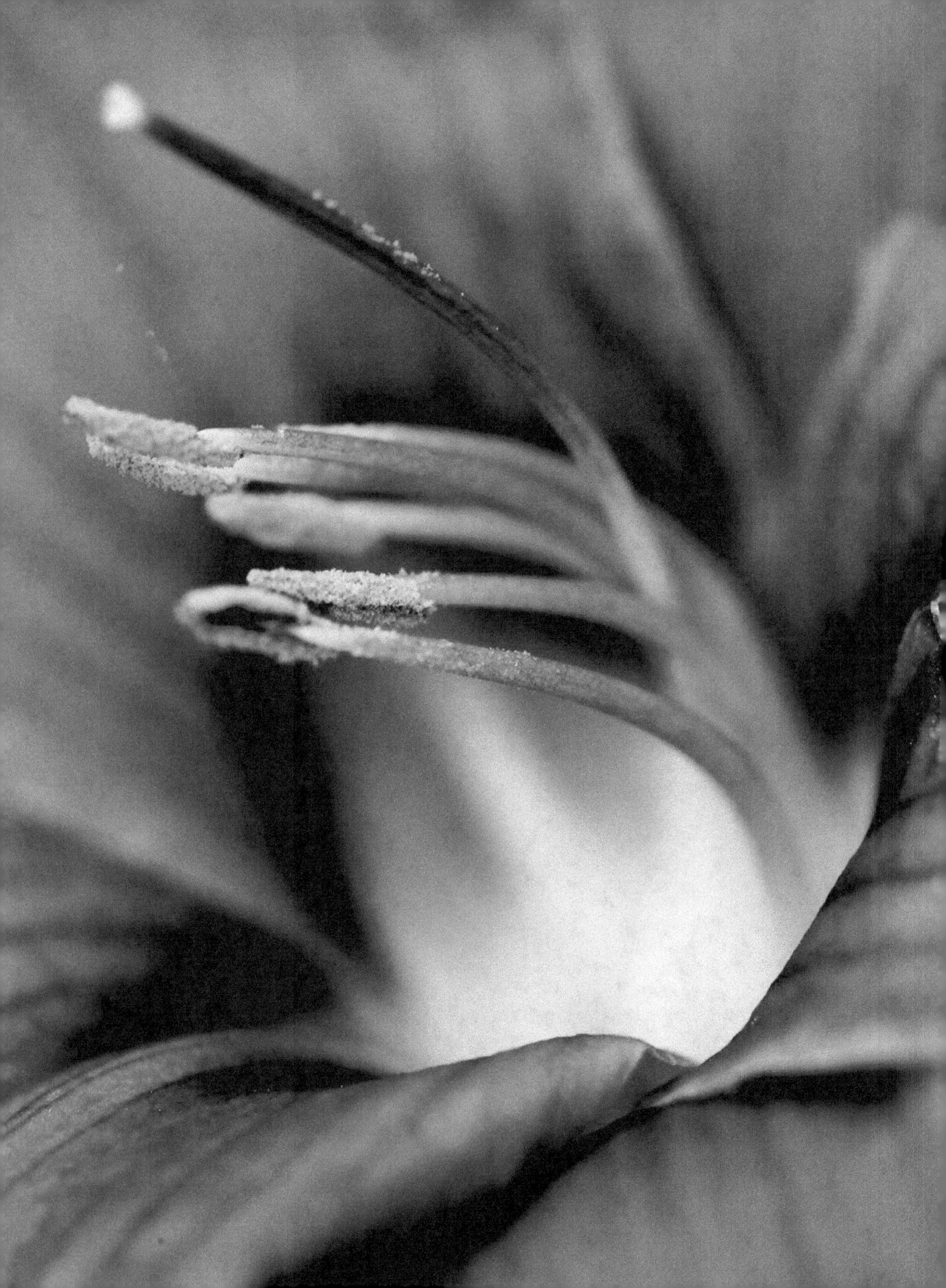

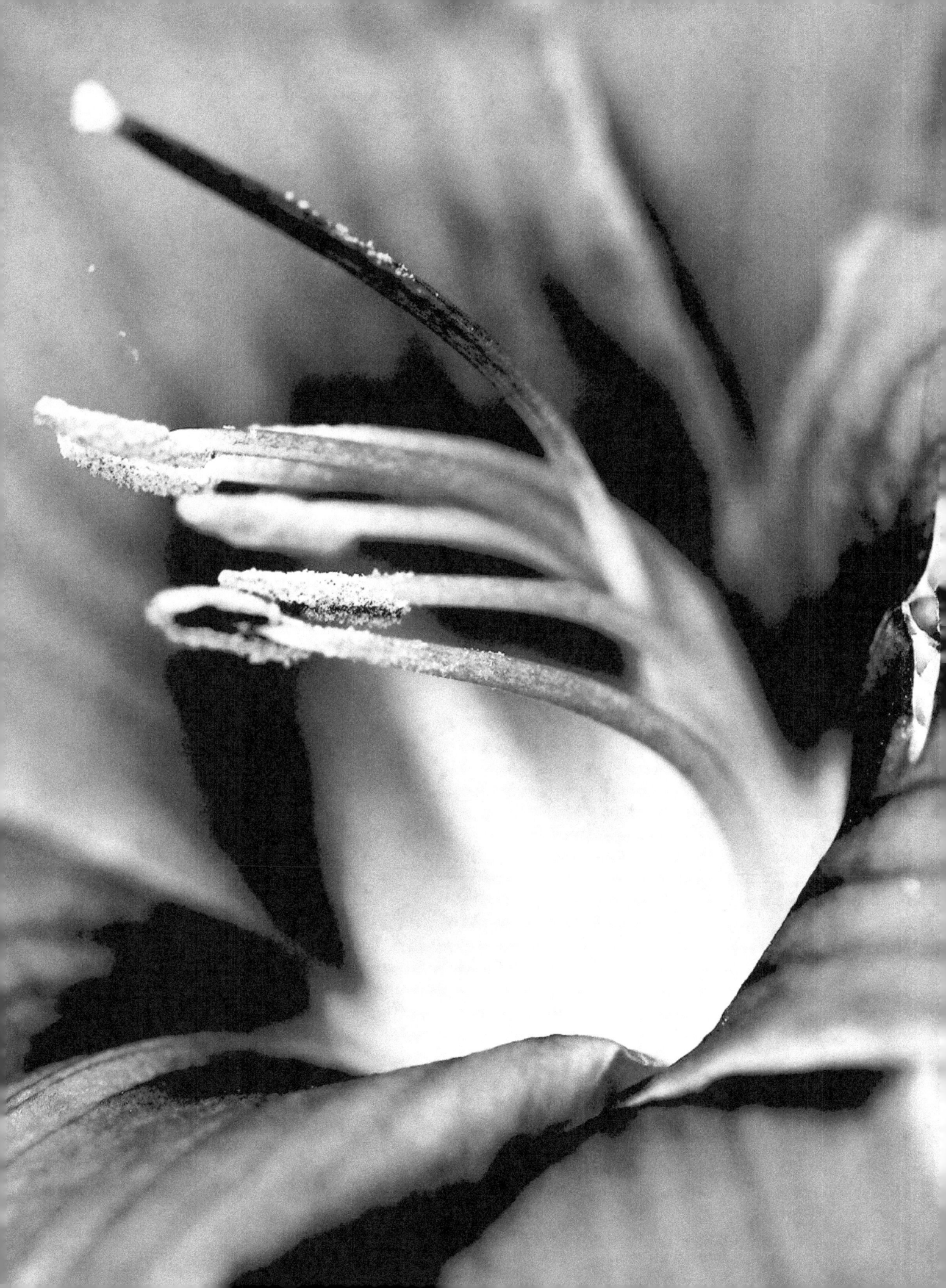

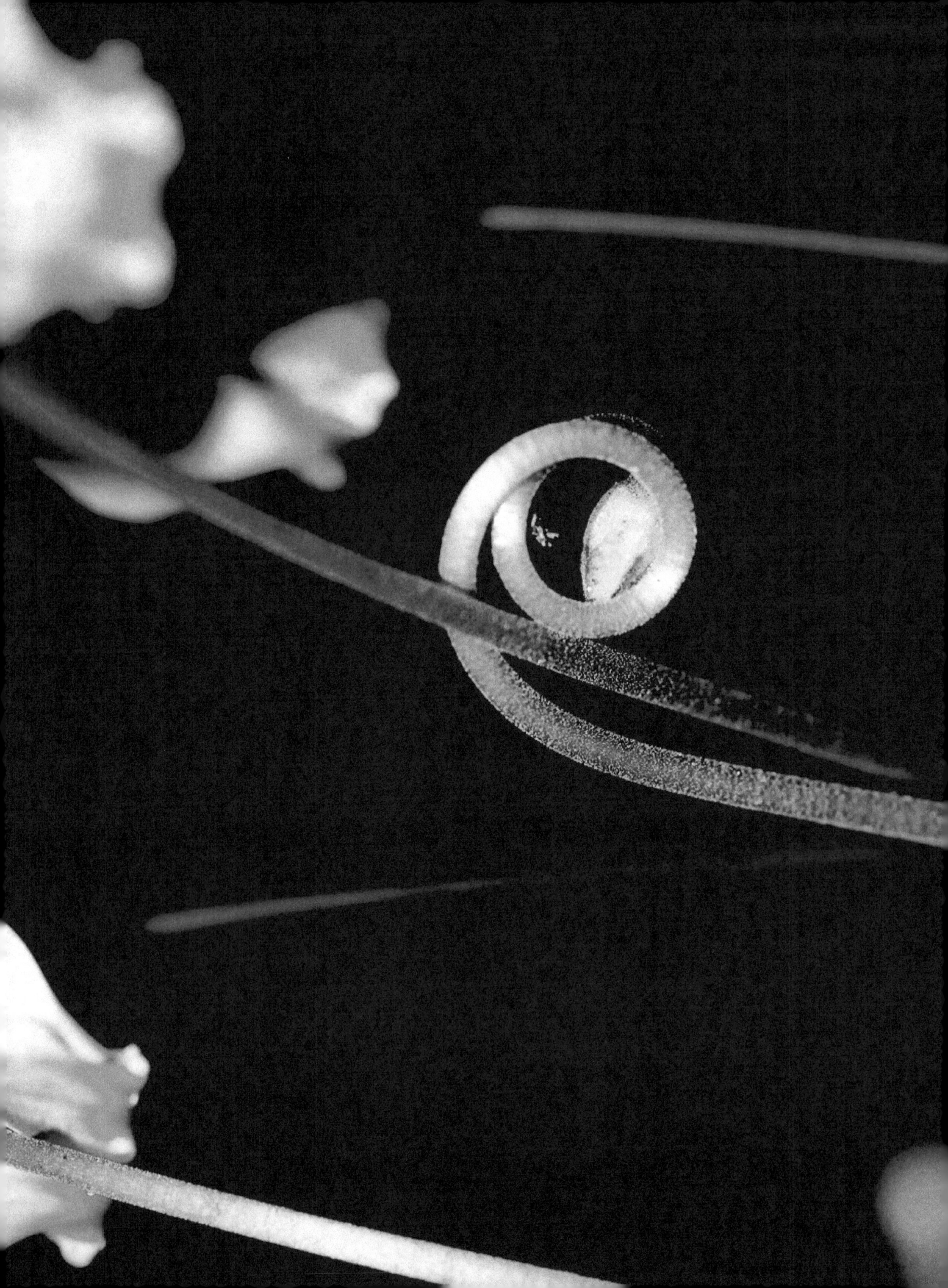

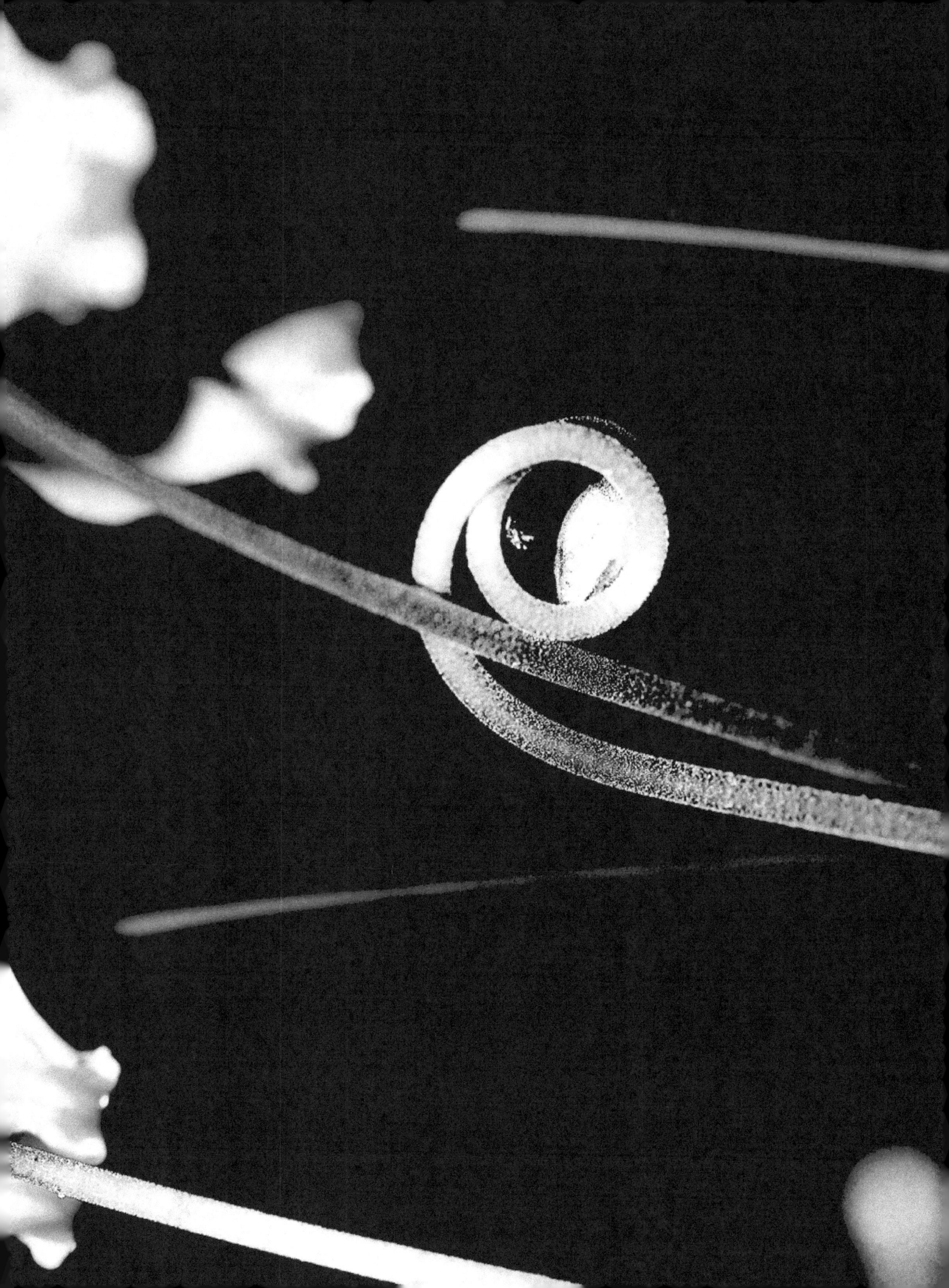

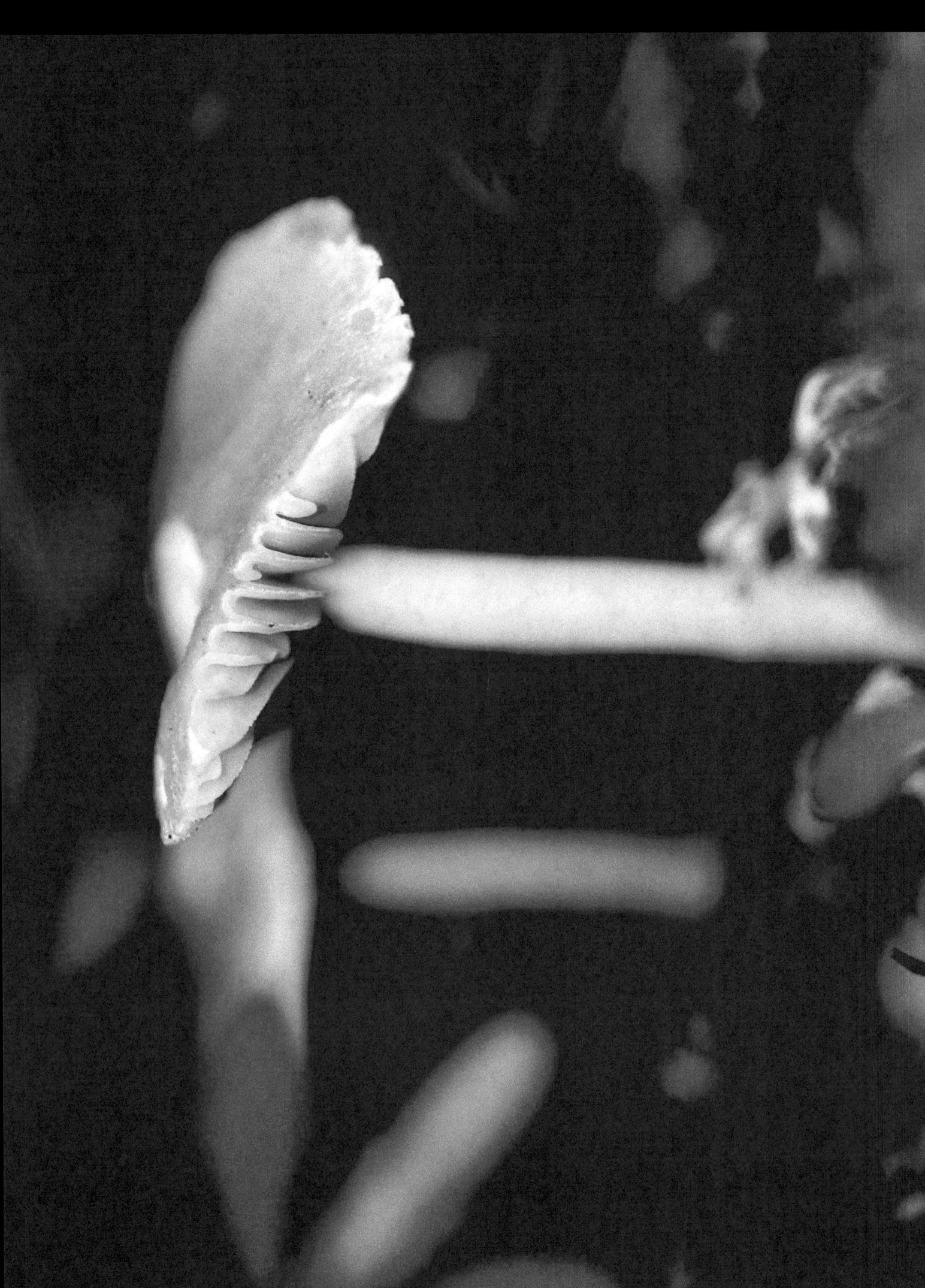

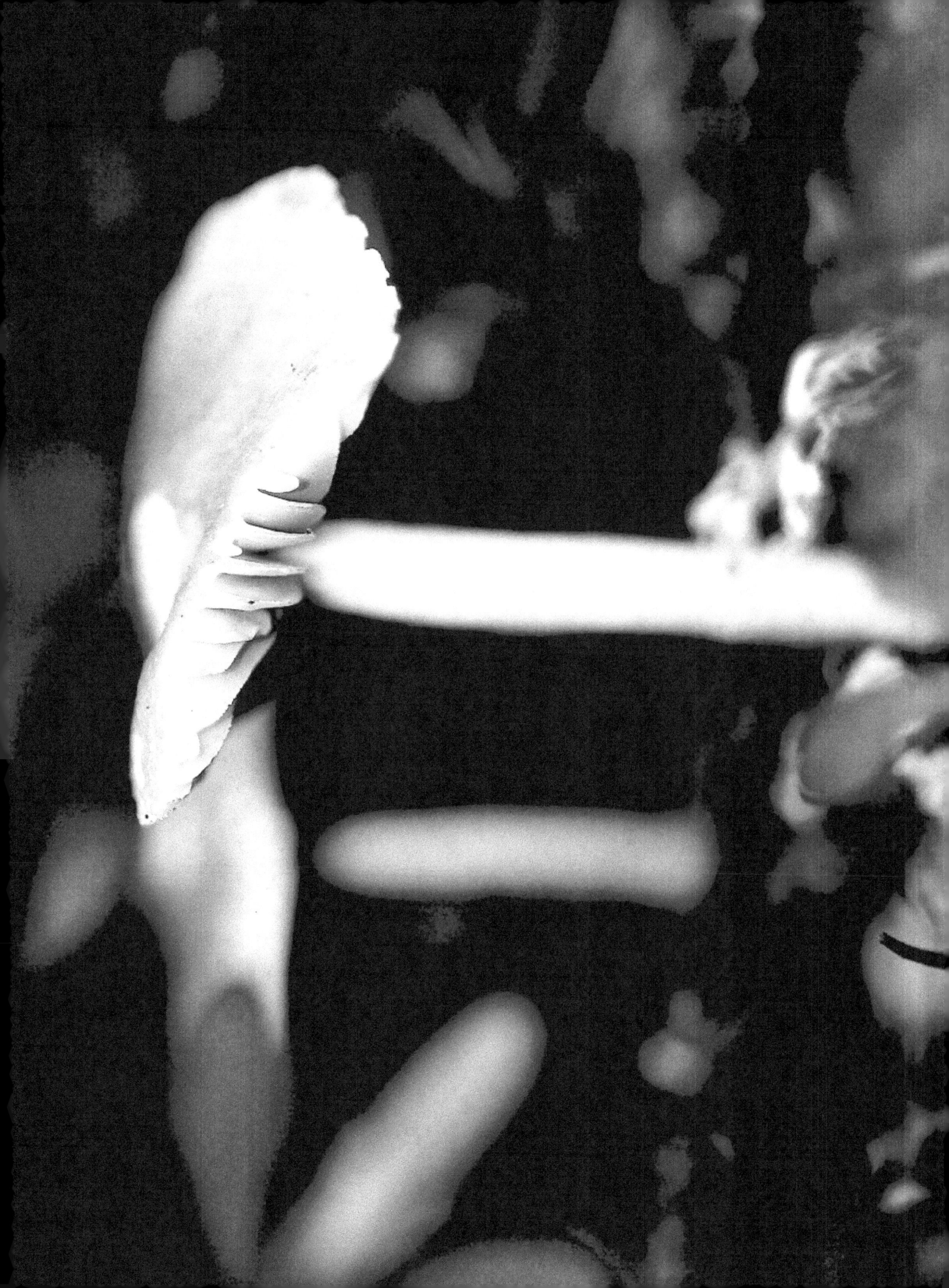

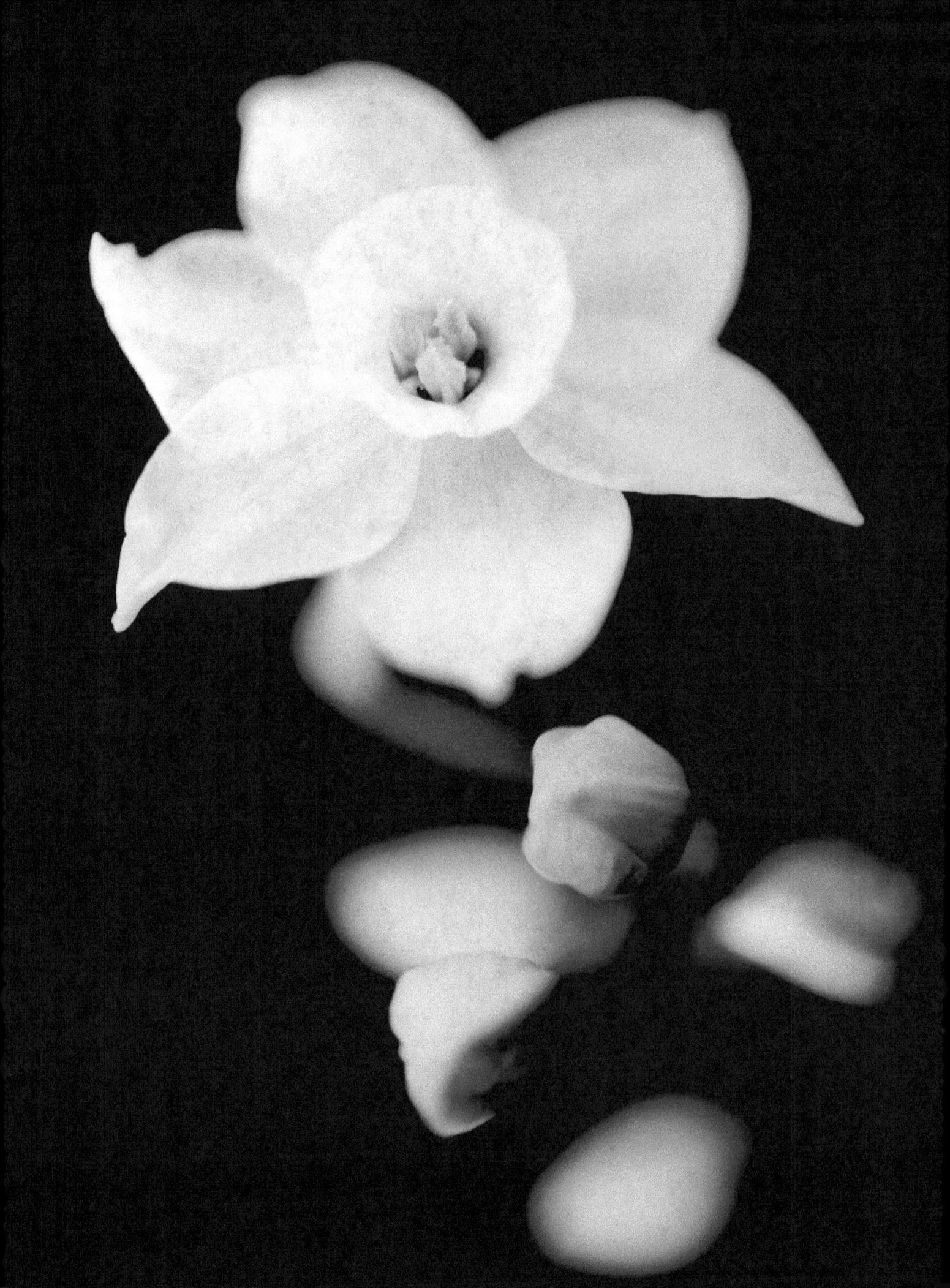

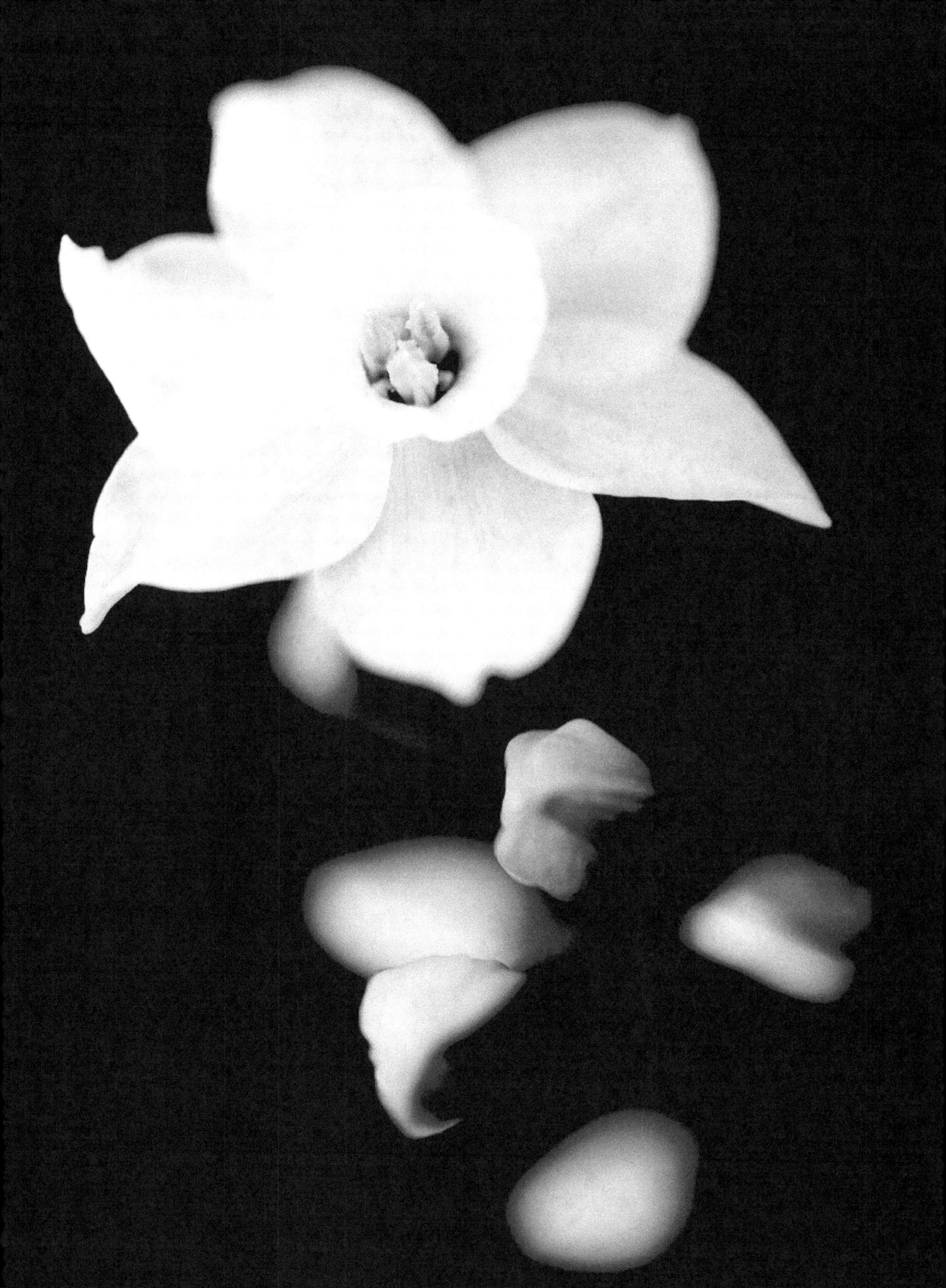

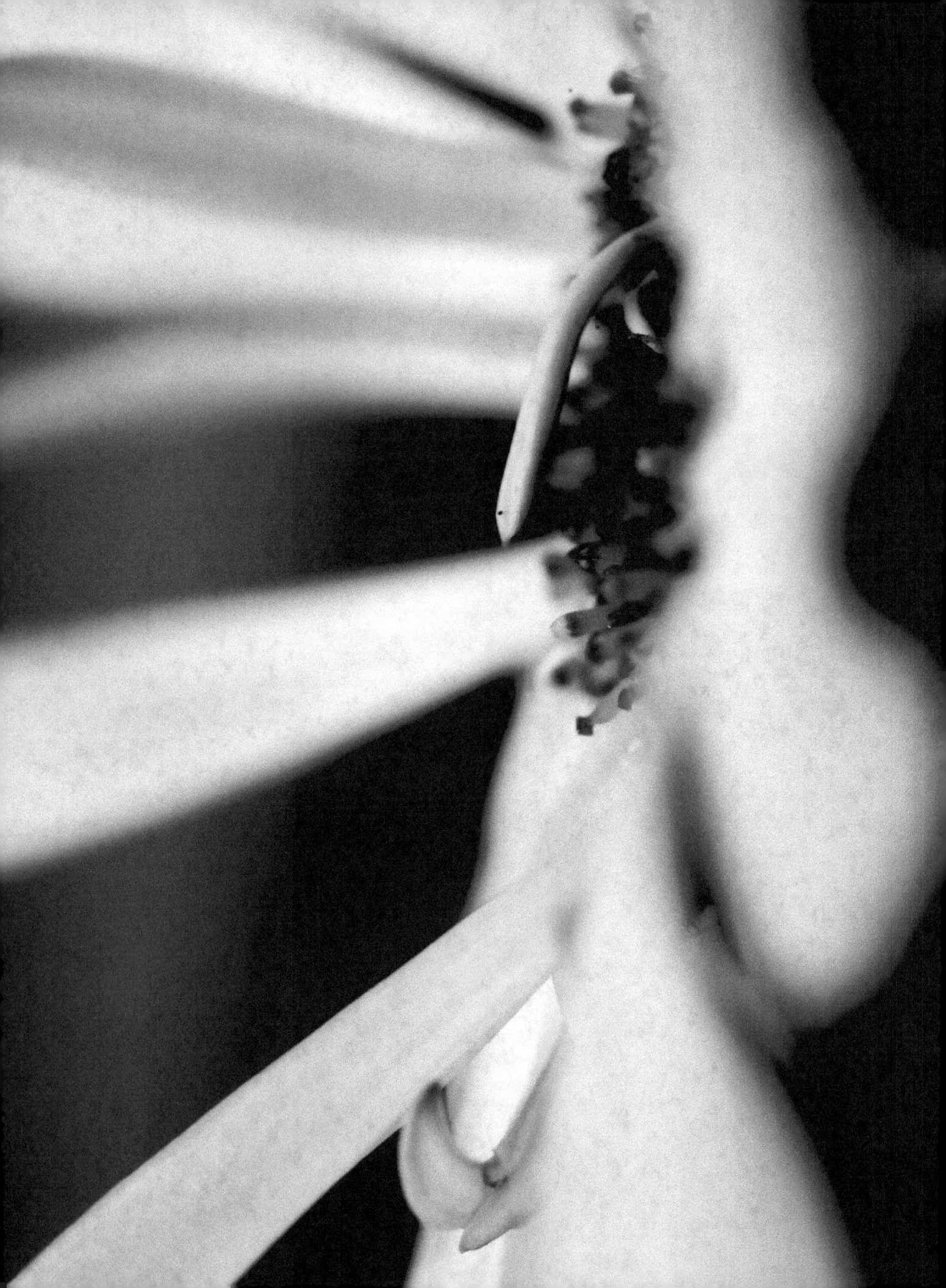

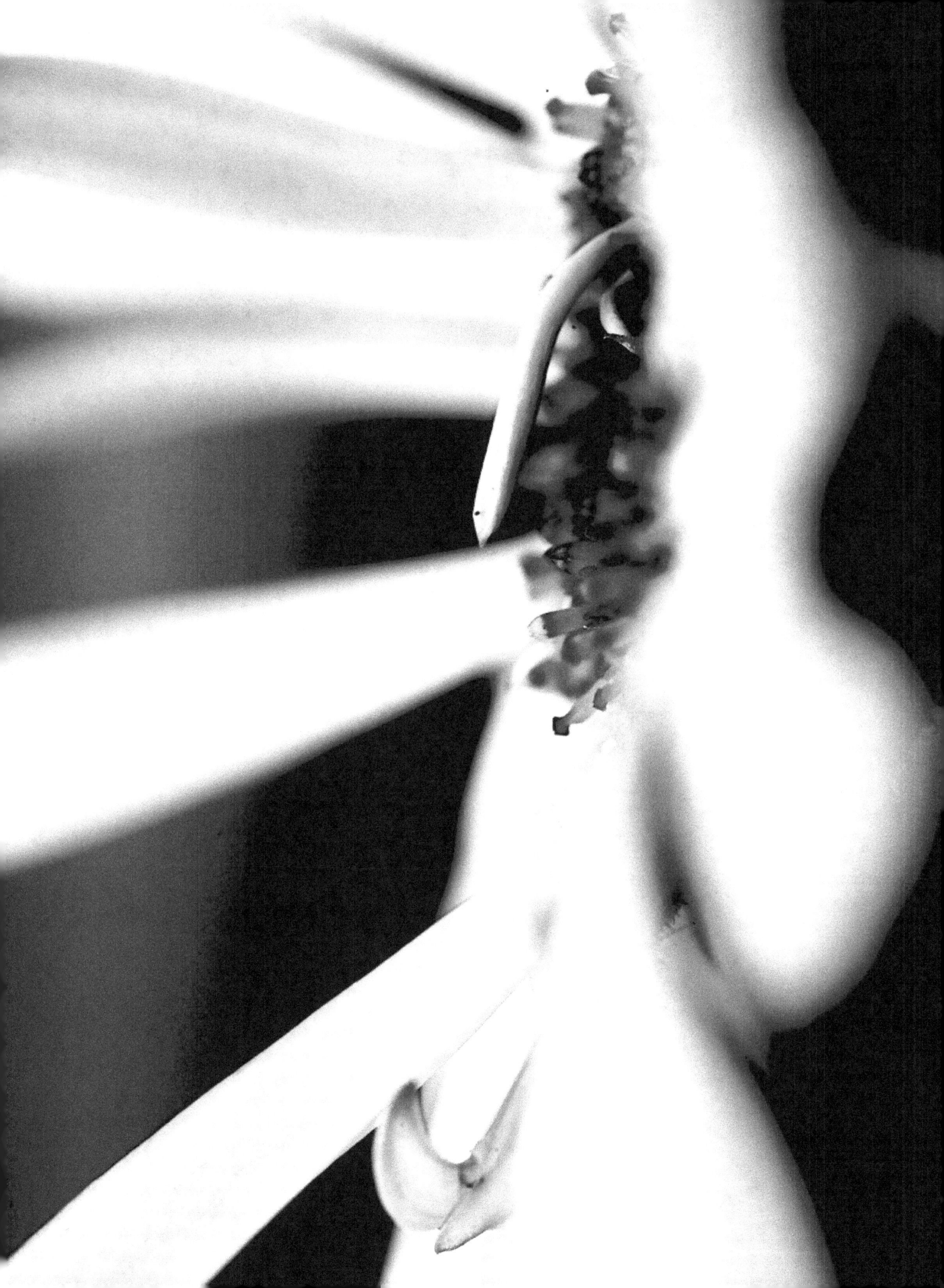

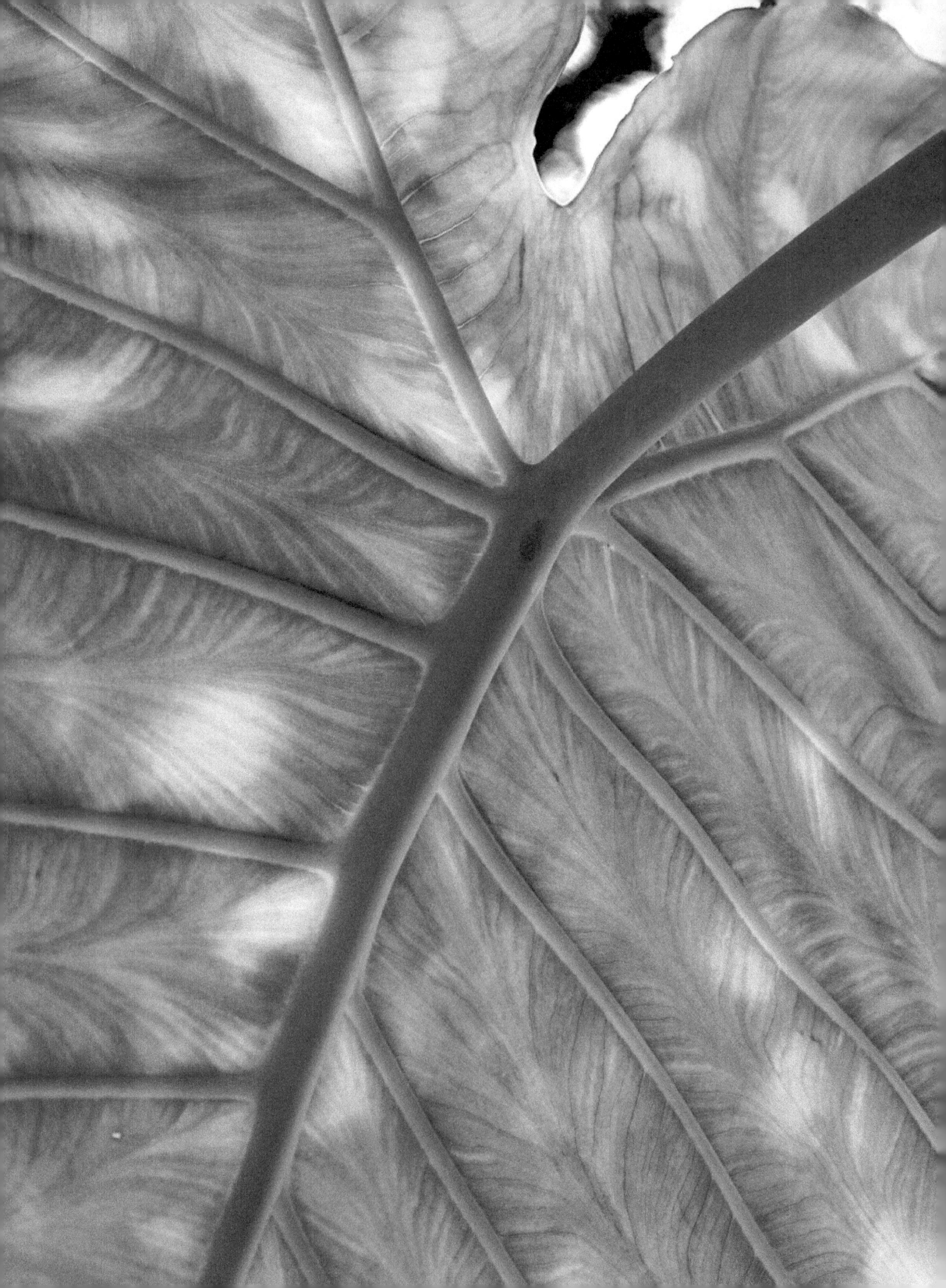

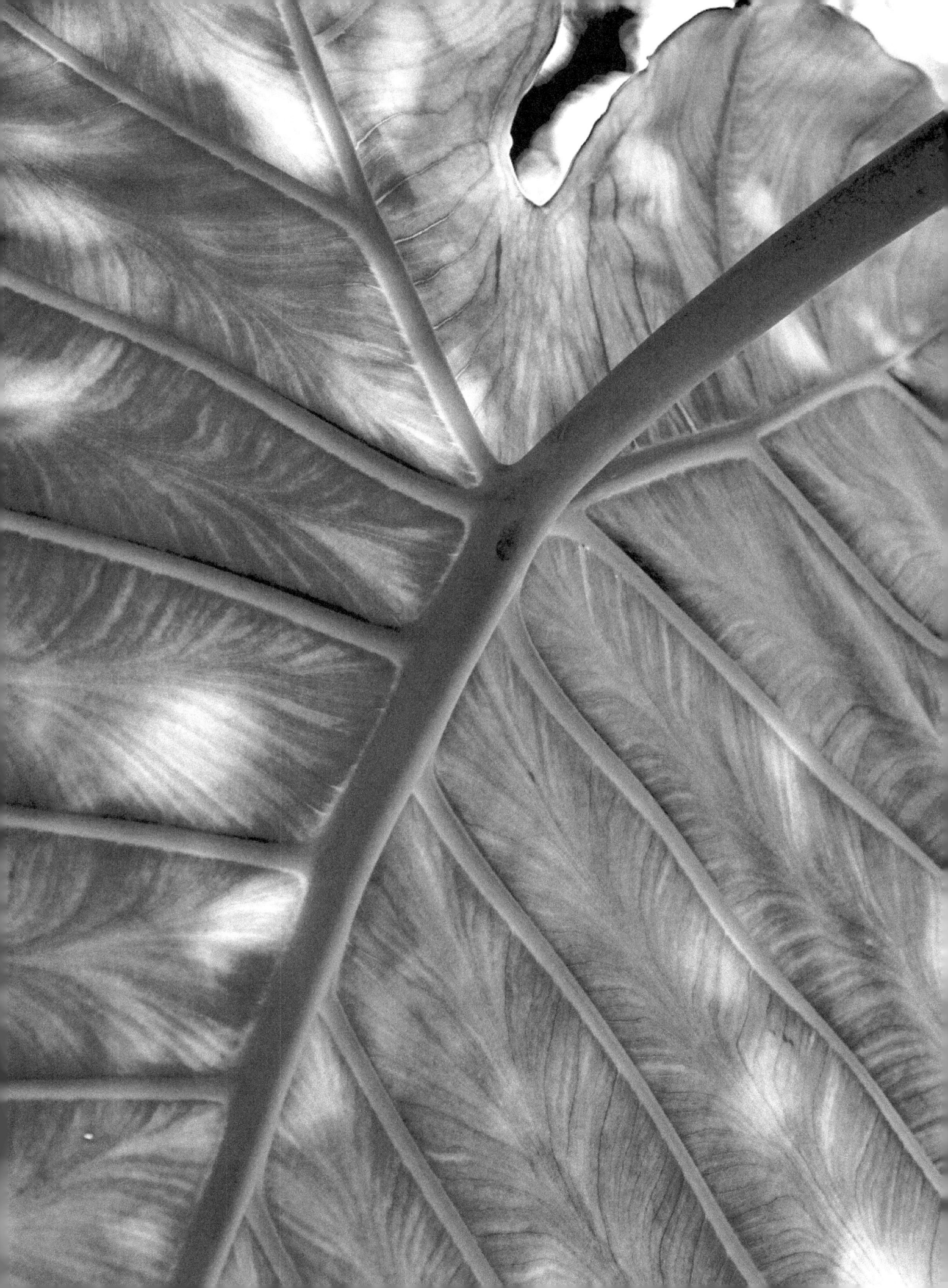

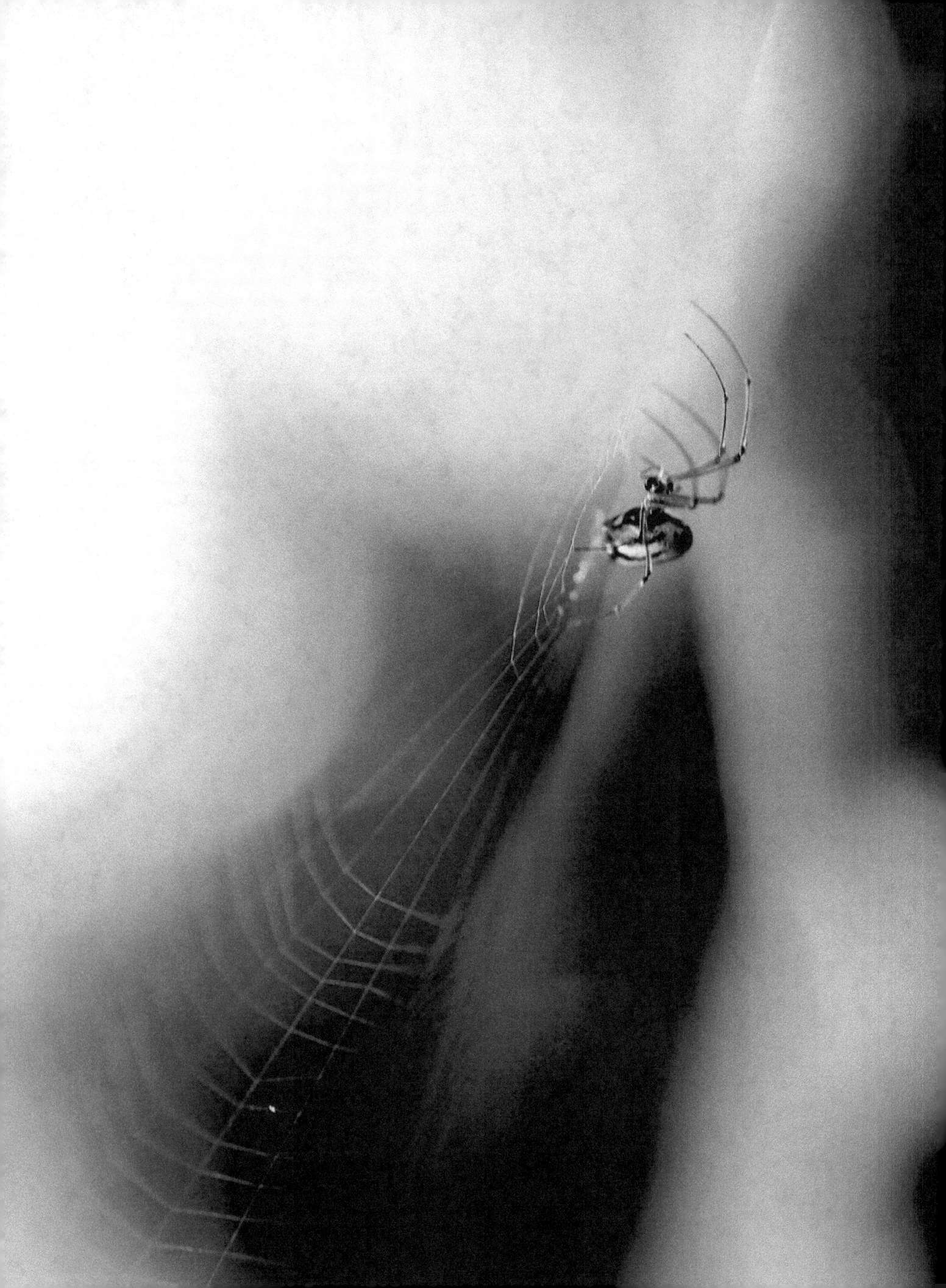

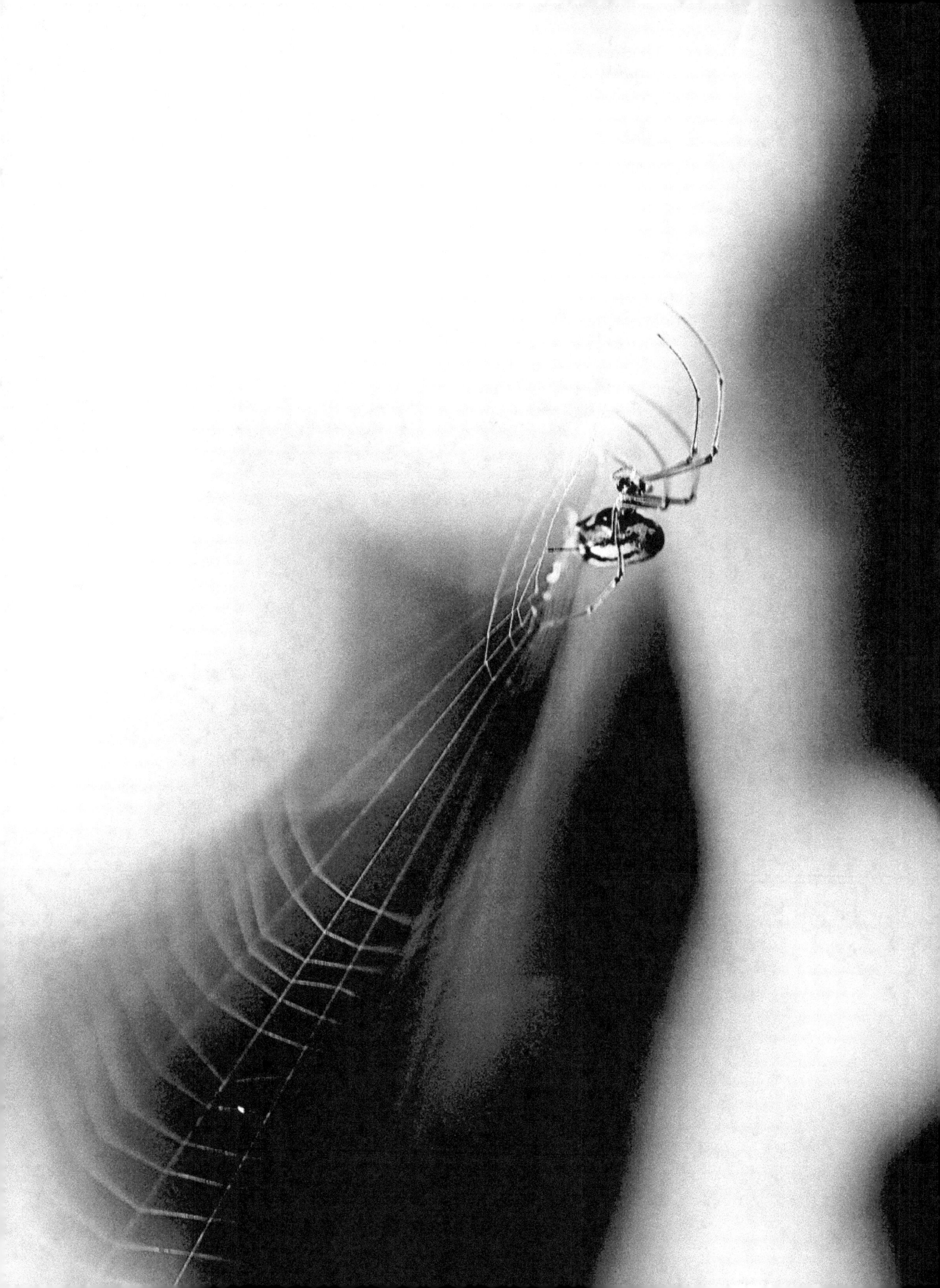

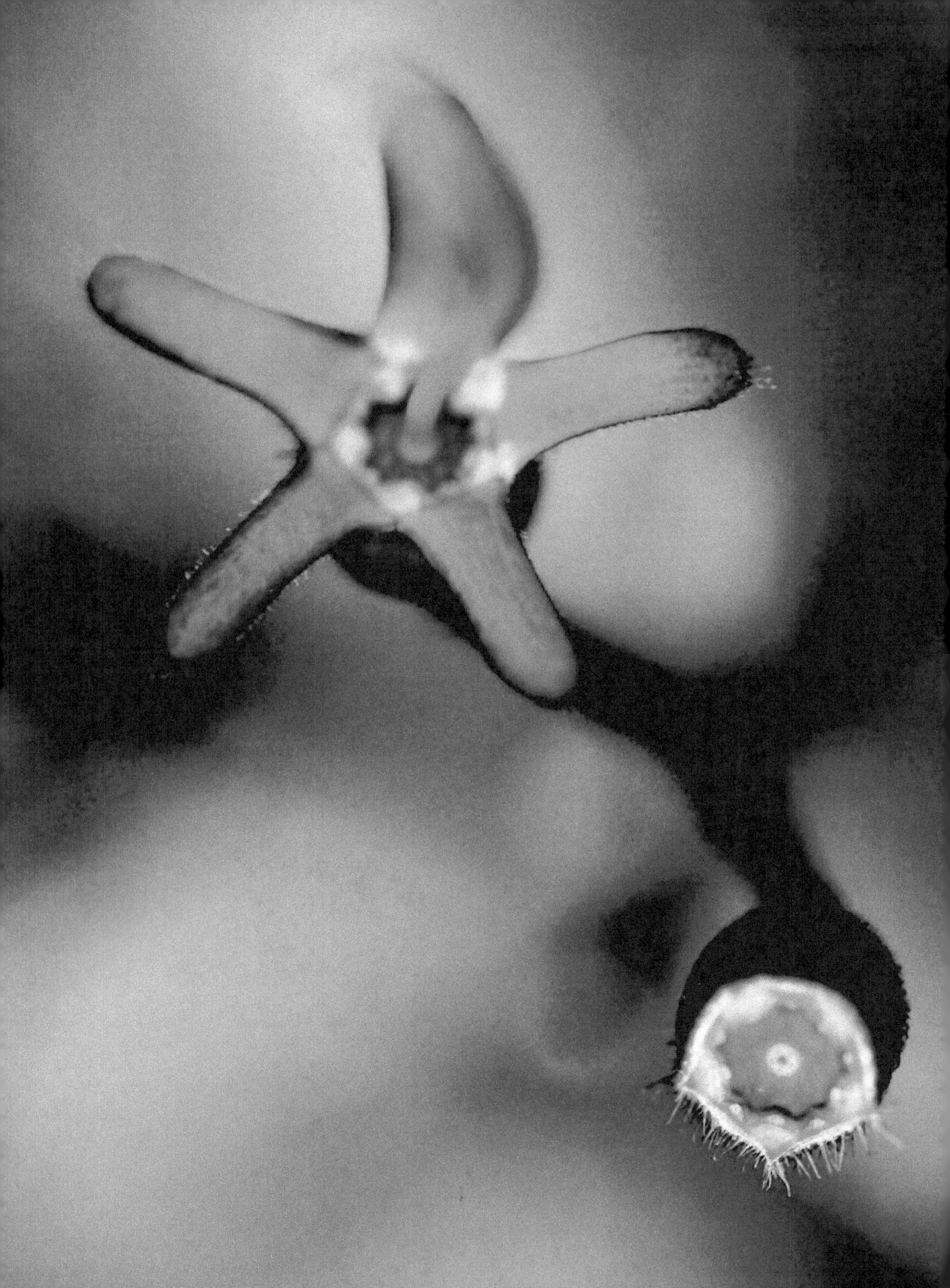

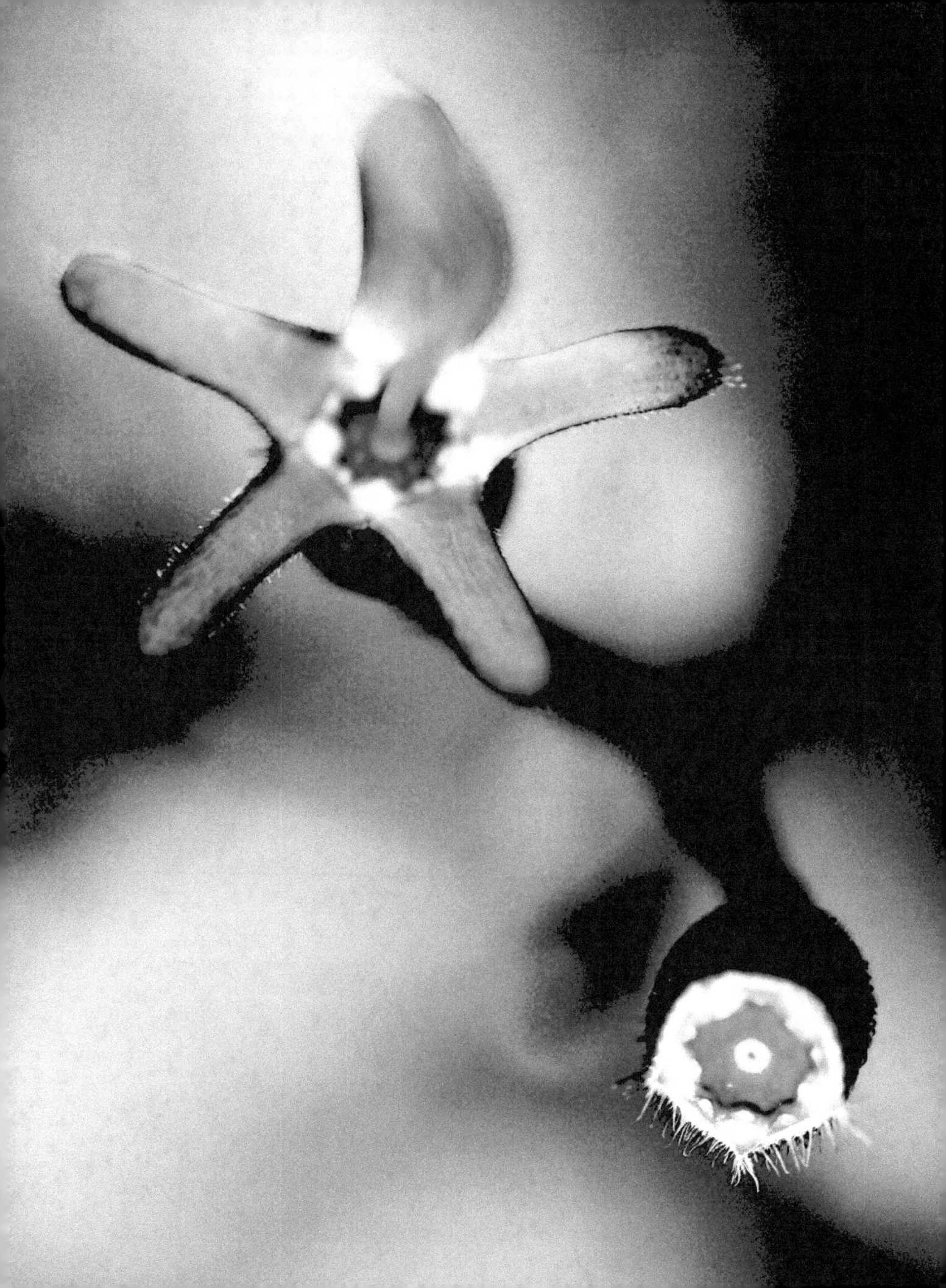

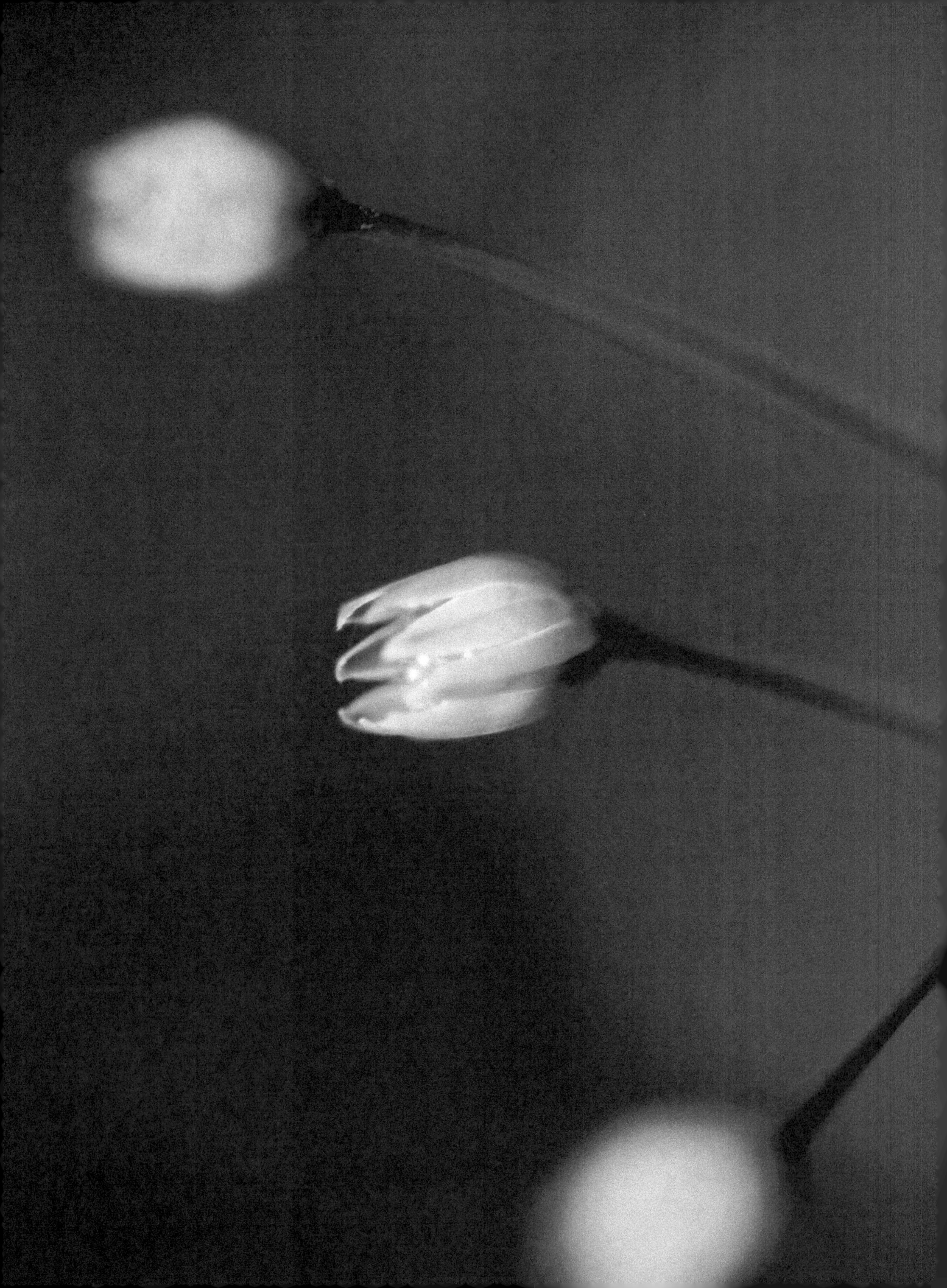

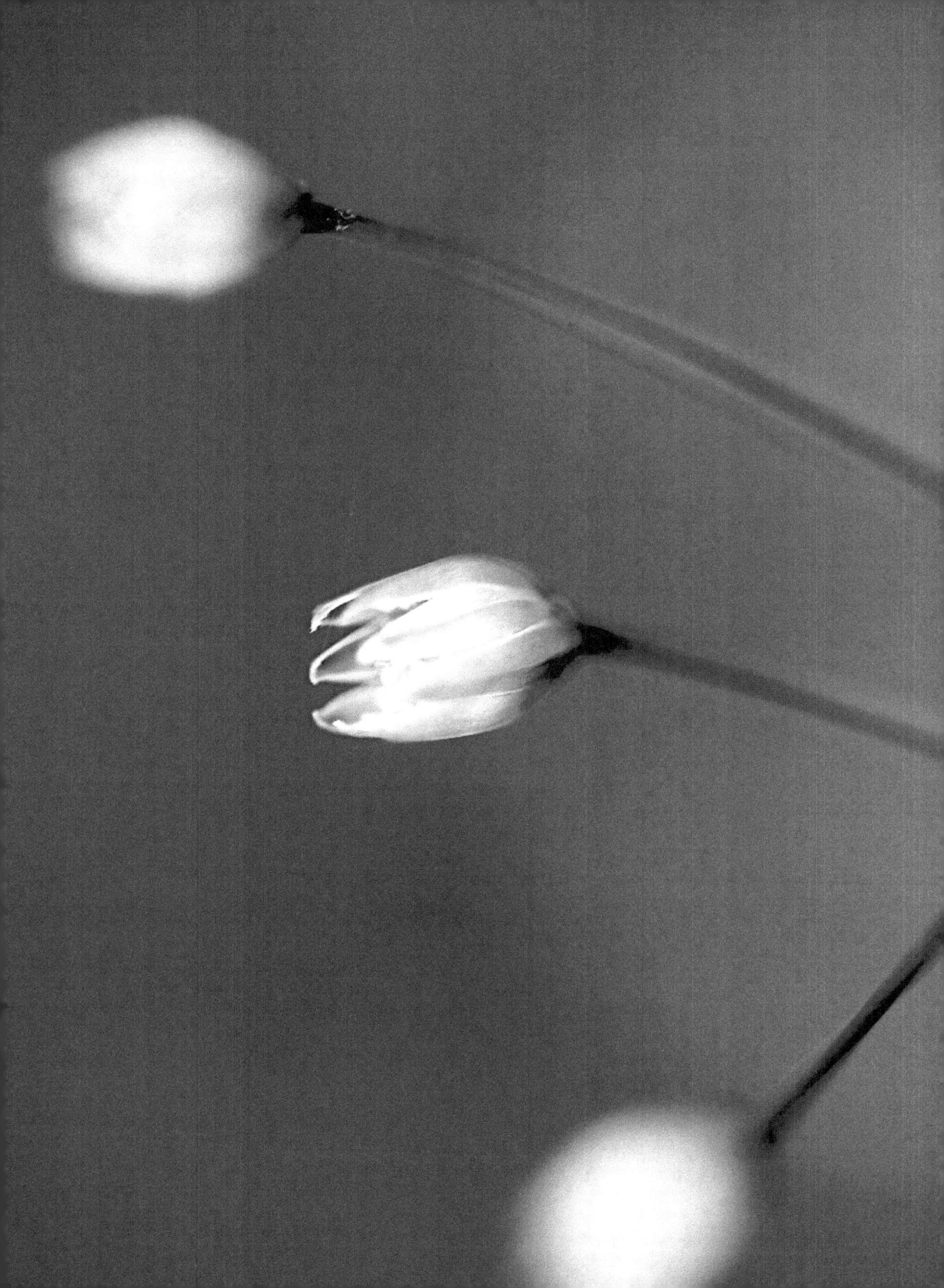

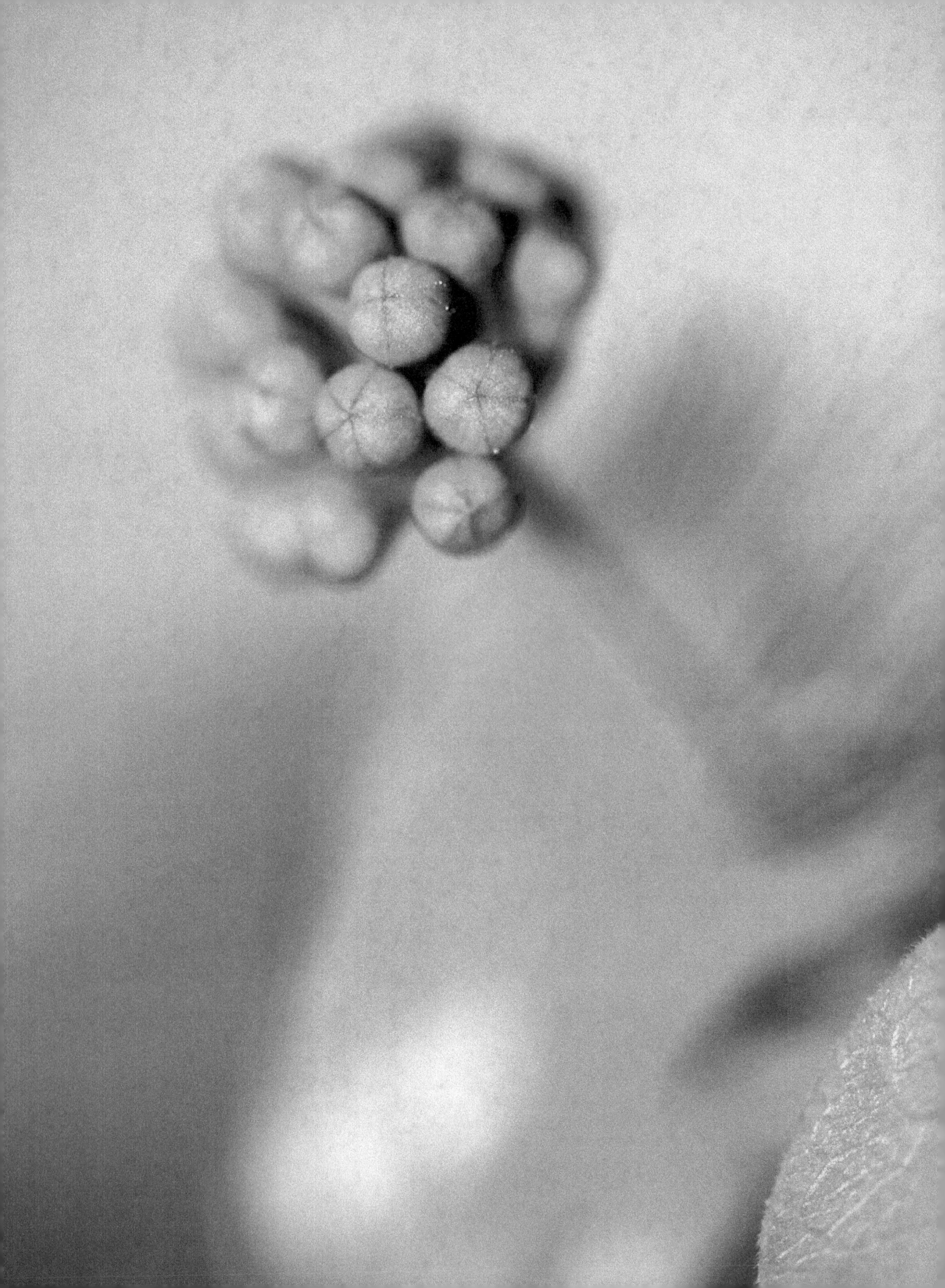

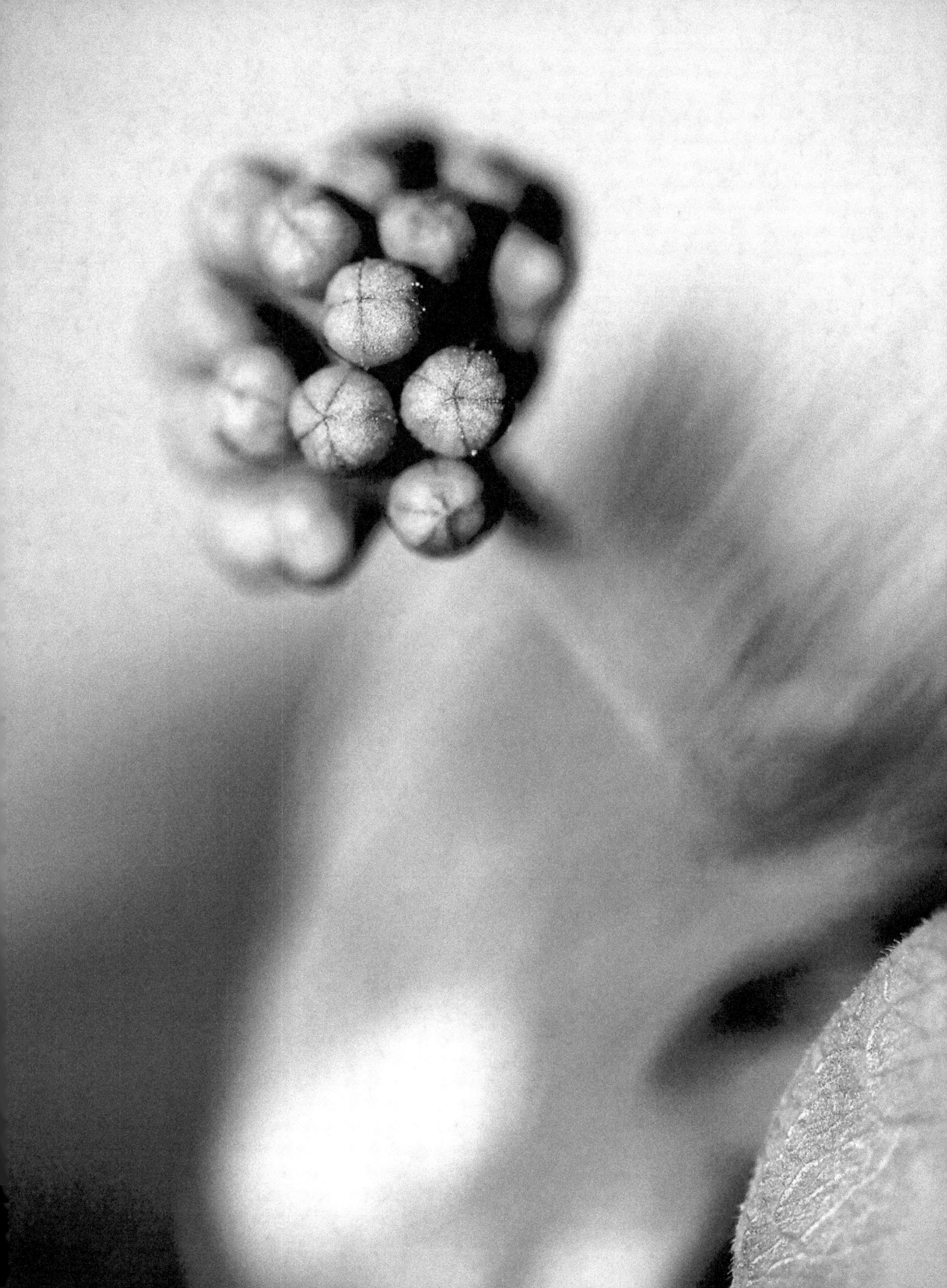

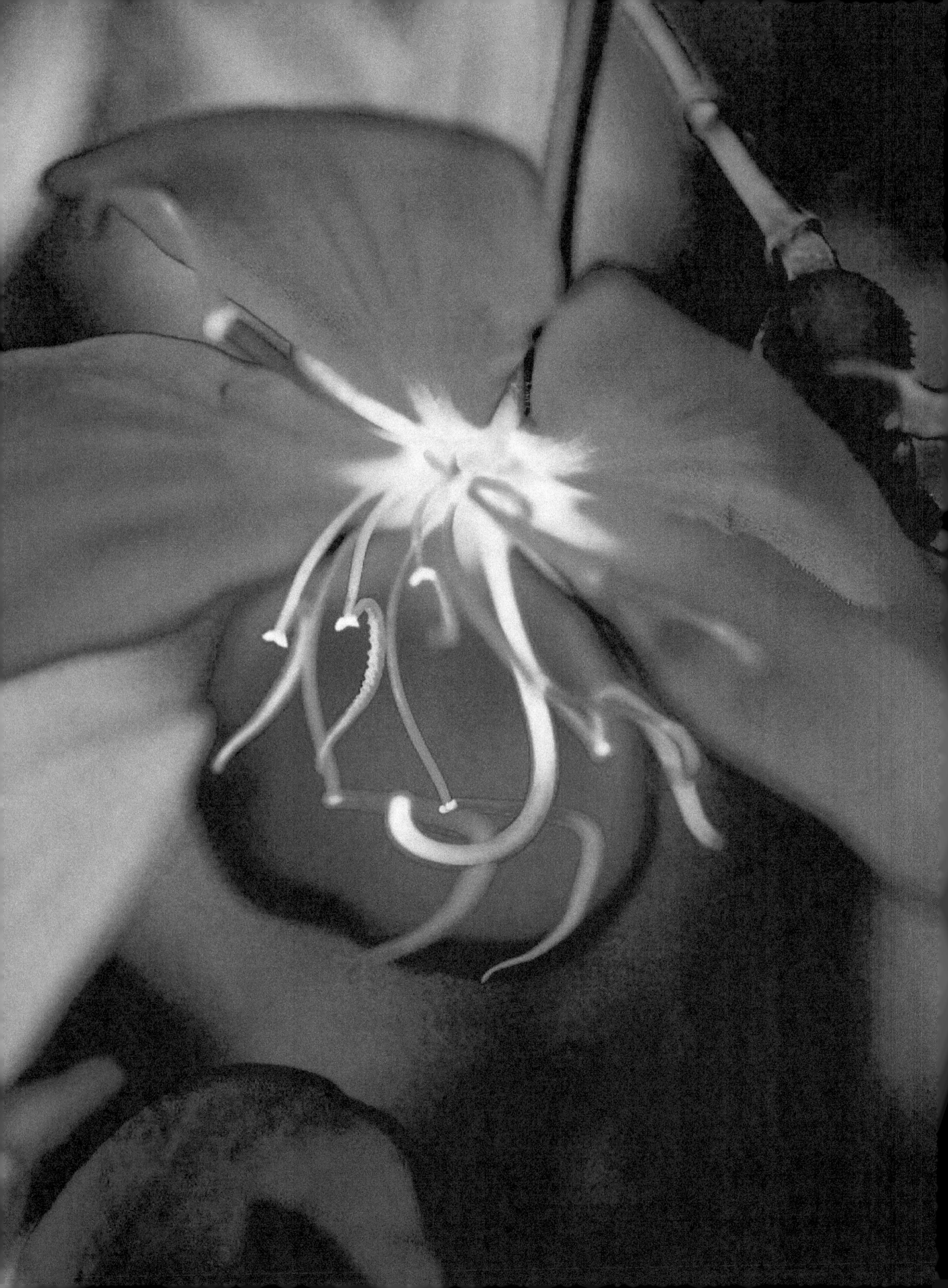

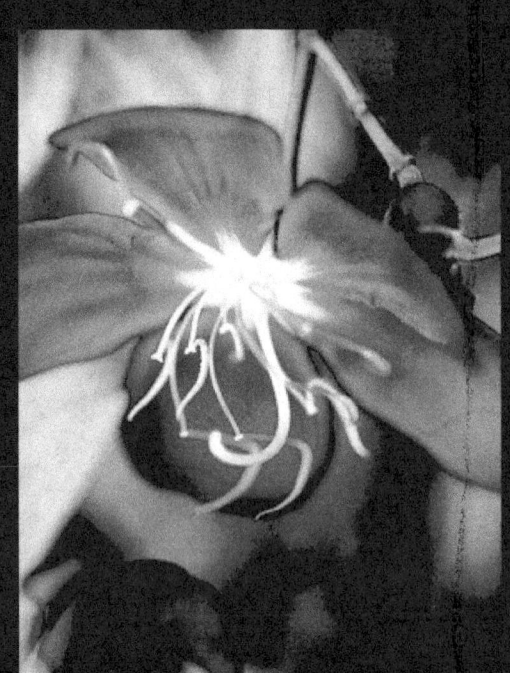

Fade To Black

by J.A. Cook

www.ingramcontent.com/pod-product-compliance
Lightning Source LLC
Chambersburg PA
CBHW080230200526
45166CB00022B/2567